Twelfth Night / What You Will

By William Shakespeare

Edited by Julien Coallier

Copyright Julien Coallier 2012

All Rights Reserved.

Scenes

Act I – Page 7

Scene 1: Duke Orsino's palace.

Scene 2: The sea-coast.

Scene 3: Olivia's house.

Scene 4: Duke Orsino's palace.

Scene 5: Olivia's house.

Act II – Page 43

Scene 1: The sea-coast.

Scene 2: A street.

Scene 3: Olivia's house.

Scene 4: Duke Orsino's palace.

Scene 5: Olivia's garden.

Act III – Page 81

Scene 1: Olivia's garden.

Scene 2: Olivia's house.

Scene 3: A street.

Scene 4: Olivia's garden.

Act IV – 123

Scene 1: Before Olivia's house.

Scene 2: Olivia's house.

Scene 3: Olivia's garden.

Act V – 139

Scene 1: Before Olivia's house.

Characters

Antonio (A sea captain, friend to Sebastain)

Captain (Friend to Viola)

Curio (Gentleman attending on the Duke)

Fabian (Servant to Olivia)

Feste (A clown, servant to Olivia)

First Officer

Malvolio (Steward to Olivia)

Maria (Olivia's woman)

Olivia

Orsino (Duke of Illyria)

Priest

Sebastian (Brother to Viola)

Second Officer

Servant

Sir Andrew Aguecheek

Sir Toby Belch (Uncle to Olivia)

Valentine (Gentleman attending on the Duke)

Viola

Act I, Scene 1

Duke Orsino's palace.

(Duke Orsino, Curio, and other Lords enter with Musicians attending)

Orsino: If music be the food of love, play on; give me excess of it, that surfeiting, the appetite may sicken, and so die that strain again!

It had a dying fall; Oh it came over my ear like the sweet sound that breathes upon a bank of violets, stealing and giving odour!

Enough, no more, it is not so sweet now as it was before.

Oh spirit of love! How quick and fresh art thou, that notwithstanding thy capacity receiveth as the sea, nought enters there.

Of what validity and pitch soever, but falls into abatement and low price, even in a minute, so full of shapes is fancy that it alone is high fantastical.

Curio: Will you go hunt, my lord?

Orsino: What, Curio?

Curio: The hart.

Orsino: Why so I do, the noblest that I have, oh when mine eyes did see Olivia first

Methought she purged the air of pestilence!

That instant I turned into a hart, and my desires fell and cruel hounds like, ever since pursue me.

(Valentine enters)

How now! What news from her?

Valentine: So please my lord, I might not be admitted, but from her handmaid do return this answer.

The element itself, till seven years' heat, shall not behold her face at ample view.

Like a cloistress she will as veiled walk, and water once a day her chamber round with eye-offending brine; all this to season a brother's dead love which she would keep fresh and lasting in her sad remembrance.

Orsino: Oh she that hath a heart of that fine frame

To pay this debt of love but to a brother, how will she love, when the rich golden shaft hath killed the flock of all affections else that live in her.

When liver, brain and heart, these sovereign thrones, are all supplied, and filled, her sweet perfections with one self King is made!

Away before me to sweet beds of flowers, love-thoughts lie rich when canopied with bowers.

(Exeunt)

Act I, Scene 2

The sea-coast.

(Viola, a Captain, and Sailors enter)

Viola: What country, friends, is this?

Captain: This is Illyria, lady.

Viola: And what should I do in Illyria?

My brother he is in Elysium.

Perchance he is not drowned, what think you, sailors?

Captain: It is perchance that you yourself were saved.

Viola: Oh my poor brother! And so perchance may he be.

Captain: True, madam, and to comfort you with chance, assure yourself, after our ship did split, when you and those poor number saved with you hung on our driving boat, I saw your brother most provident in peril, who bind himself; courage and hope both teaching him the practice.

To a strong master that lived upon the sea, where like Arion on the dolphin's back, I saw him hold acquaintance with the waves; so long as I could see.

Viola: For saying so, there's gold.

Mine own escape unfoldeth to my hope, whereto thy speech serves for authority the like of him.

Know'st thou this country?

Captain: Ay, madam, well; for I was bred and born

Not three hours' travel from this very place.

Viola: Who governs there?

Captain: A noble duke, in nature as in name.

Viola: What is the name?

Captain: Orsino.

Viola: Orsino! I have heard my father name him, he was a bachelor then.

Captain: And so is now, or was so very late, for but a month ago I went from hence, and then it was fresh in murmur; as you know, what great ones do the less will prattle of

That he did seek the love of fair Olivia.

Viola: What's she?

Captain: A virtuous maid, the daughter of a count that died some twelvemonth, since then leaving her in the protection of his son, her brother, who shortly also died.

For whose dear love they say she hath abjured the company and sight of men.

Viola: Oh that I served that lady and might not be delivered to the world till I had made mine own occasion mellow, what my estate is!

Captain: That were hard to compass, because she will admit no kind of suit, no, not the duke's.

Viola: There is a fair behavior in thee, captain, and though that nature with a beauteous wall doth often close in pollution, yet of thee I will believe thou hast a mind that suits with this, thy fair and outward character

I pray to thee, and I'll pay thee bounteously, conceal me what I am, and be my aid for such disguise as happily shall become the form of my intent.

I'll serve this duke, thou shall present me as an eunuch to him that it may be worth thy pains; for I can sing and speak to him in many sorts of music that will allow me very worth his service.

What else may hap to time I will commit, only shape thou thy silence to my wit.

Captain: Be you his eunuch, and your mute I'll be, when my tongue blabs then let mine eyes not see.

Viola: I thank thee, lead me on.

(Exeunt)

Act I, Scene 3

Olivia's house.

(Sir Toby Belch and Maria enter)

Sir Toby Belch: What a plague means my niece, to take the death of her brother thus?

I am sure care's an enemy to life.

Maria: By my troth Sir Toby, you must come in earlier of nights.

Your cousin, my lady, takes great exceptions to your ill hours.

Sir Toby Belch: Why, let her except, before excepted.

Maria: Ay, but you must confine yourself within the modest limits of order.

Sir Toby Belch: Confine! I'll confine myself no finer than I am.

These clothes are good enough to drink in; and so be these boots too; and if they be not, let them hang themselves in their own straps.

Maria: That quaffing and drinking will undo you, I heard my lady talk of it yesterday; and of a foolish knight that you brought in one night here to be her wooer.

Sir Toby Belch: Who, Sir Andrew Aguecheek?

Maria: Ay, he.

Sir Toby Belch: He's as tall a man as any is in Illyria.

Maria: What's that to the purpose?

Sir Toby Belch: Why, he has three thousand ducats a year.

Maria: Ay, but he'll have but a year in all these ducats, he's a very fool and a prodigal.

Sir Toby Belch: Fie, that you'll say so! He plays of the violin, and speaks three or four languages, word for word without book; and hath all the good gifts of nature.

Maria: He hath indeed, almost natural, for besides that he's a fool, he's a great quarreller: and he hath the gift of a coward to allay the gust he hath in quarrelling; it is thought among the prudent he would quickly have the gift of a grave.

Sir Toby Belch: By this hand, they are scoundrels and subtractors that say so of him.

Who are they?

Maria: They that add, moreover, he's drunk nightly in your company.

Sir Toby Belch: With drinking healths to my niece, I'll drink to her as long as there is a passage in my throat and drink in Illyria.

He's a coward and a coystrill that will not drink to my niece till his brains turn of the toe like a parish-top.

What wench! Castiliano vulgo! For here comes Sir Andrew Agueface.

(Sir Andrew enters)

Sir Andrew Aguecheek: Sir Toby Belch! How now, Sir Toby Belch!

Sir Toby Belch: Sweet Sir Andrew!

Sir Andrew Aguecheek: Bless you, fair shrew.

Maria: And you too, sir.

Sir Toby Belch: Accost, Sir Andrew, accost.

Sir Andrew Aguecheek: What's that?

Sir Toby Belch: My niece's chambermaid.

Sir Andrew Aguecheek: Good Mistress Accost, I desire better acquaintance.

Maria: My name is Mary, sir.

Sir Andrew Aguecheek: Good Mistress Mary Accost.

Sir Toby Belch: You mistake, knight, accost is front her, board her, woo her, assail her.

Sir Andrew Aguecheek: By my troth, I would not undertake her in this company.

Is that the meaning of accost?

Maria: Fare you well, gentlemen.

Sir Toby Belch: An thou let part so, Sir Andrew, would thou mightst never draw sword again.

Sir Andrew Aguecheek: And you part so, mistress, I would, I might never draw sword again.

Fair lady, do you think you have fools in hand?

Maria: Sir, I have not you by the hand.

Sir Andrew Aguecheek: Merrily, but you shall have, and here's my hand.

Maria: Now sir, thought is free, I pray you bring your hand to the buttery-bar and let it drink.

Sir Andrew Aguecheek: Wherefore, sweet-heart? What's your metaphor?

Maria: It's dry, sir.

Sir Andrew Aguecheek: Why, I think so: I am not such an ass but I can keep my hand dry. But what's your jest?

Maria: A dry jest, sir.

Sir Andrew Aguecheek: Are you full of them?

Maria: Ay, sir, I have them at my fingers' ends, merrily, now I let go your hand, I am barren.

(Exits)

Sir Toby Belch: Oh knight, thou lackest a cup of canary.

When did I see thee so put down?

Sir Andrew Aguecheek: Never in your life, I think, unless you see canary put me down. Methinks sometimes I have no more wit than a Christian or an ordinary man has, but I am a great eater of beef, and I believe that does harm to my wit.

Sir Toby Belch: No question.

Sir Andrew Aguecheek: And I thought that, I would forswear it.

I'll ride home to-morrow, Sir Toby.

Sir Toby Belch: Why, my dear knight?

Sir Andrew Aguecheek: What is Why? Do or not do? I would I had bestowed that time in the tongues that I have in fencing, dancing and bear-baiting.

Oh had I but followed the arts!

Sir Toby Belch: Then hadst thou had an excellent head of hair.

Sir Andrew Aguecheek: Why, would that have mended my hair?

Sir Toby Belch: Past question; for thou seest it will not curl by nature.

Sir Andrew Aguecheek: But it becomes me well enough, does't not?

Sir Toby Belch: Excellent; it hangs like flax on a distaff, and I hope to see a housewife take thee between her legs and spin it off.

Sir Andrew Aguecheek: Faith, I'll home to-morrow, Sir Toby: your niece will not be seen, or if she be, it's four to one she'll none of me.

The count himself here hard by woos her.

Sir Toby Belch: She'll none of the count.

She'll not match above her degree, neither in estate, years, nor wit; have heard her swear it.

Tut, there's life in it, man.

Sir Andrew Aguecheek: I'll stay a month longer. I am a fellow of the strangest mind in the world; I delight in masques and revels sometimes altogether.

Sir Toby Belch: Art thou good at these kickshawses, knight?

Sir Andrew Aguecheek: As any man in Illyria, whatsoever he be, under the degree of my betters; and yet I will not compare with an old man.

Sir Toby Belch: What is thy excellence in a galliard, knight?

Sir Andrew Aguecheek: Faith, I can cut a caper.

Sir Toby Belch: And I can cut the mutton to it.

Sir Andrew Aguecheek: And I think I have the back-trick simply as strong as any man in Illyria.

Sir Toby Belch: Wherefore are these things hid? Wherefore have these gifts a curtain before them? Are they like to take dust, like Mistress Mall's picture?

Why dost thou not go to church in a galliard and come home in a coranto?

My very walk should be a jig, I would not so much as make water but in a sink-a-pace.

What dost thou mean? Is it a world to hide virtues in?

I did think, by the excellent constitution of thy leg, it was formed under the star of a galliard.

Sir Andrew Aguecheek: Ay, it is strong, and it does indifferent well in a flame-coloured stock. Shall we set about some revels?

Sir Toby Belch: What shall we do else? were we not born under Taurus?

Sir Andrew Aguecheek: Taurus! That's sides and heart.

Sir Toby Belch: No sir, it is legs and thighs.

Let me see the caper, ha!

Higher, ha, ha! excellent!

(Exeunt)

Act I, Scene 4

Duke Orsino's palace.

(Valentine and Viola enter in man's attire)

Valentine: If the duke continue these favours towards you, Cesario, you are like to be much advanced.

He hath known you but three days, and already you are no stranger.

Viola: You either fear his humour or my negligence, that you call in question the continuance of his love.

Is he inconstant, sir, in his favours?

Valentine: No, believe me.

Viola: I thank you. Here comes the count.

(Duke Orsino, Curio, and Attendants enter)

Orsino: Who saw Cesario, oh?

Viola: On your attendance my lord, here.

Orsino: Stand you a while aloof, Cesario, thou know'st no less but all, I have unclasped to thee the book even of my secret soul; therefore, good youth, address thy gait unto her.

Be not denied access, stand at her doors, and tell them, there thy fixed foot shall grow till thou have audience.

Viola: Sure, my noble lord, if she be so abandoned to her sorrow; as it is spoke she never will admit me.

Orsino: Be clamorous and leap all civil bounds rather than make unprofited return.

Viola: Say I do speak with her, my lord, what then?

Orsino: Oh then, unfold the passion of my love, surprise her with discourse of my dear faith.

It shall become thee well to act my woes, she will attend it better in thy youth than in a nuncio's of more grave aspect.

Viola: I think not so, my lord.

Orsino: Dear lad, believe it, for they shall yet belie thy happy years, that say thou art a man.

Diana's lip is not more smooth and rubious, thy small pipe is as the maiden's organ, shrill and sound; and all is semblative a woman's part.

I know thy constellation is right apt for this affair.

Some four or five attend him, all, if you will, for I myself am best when least in company. Prosper well in this, and thou shalt live as freely as thy lord to call his fortunes thine.

Viola: I'll do my best to woo your lady.

(From Aside)

Yet, a barful strife! Whoever I woo, myself would be his wife.

(Exeunt)

Act I, Scene 5

Olivia's house.

(Maria and Jester enter)

Maria: Nay, either tell me where thou hast been, or I will not open my lips so wide as a bristle may enter in way of thy excuse.

My lady will hang thee for thy absence.

Feste: Let her hang me: he that is well hanged in this world needs to fear no colours.

Maria: Make that good.

Feste: He shall see none to fear.

Maria: A good lenten answer, I can tell thee where that saying was born of, I fear no colours.

Feste: Where, good Mistress Mary?

Maria: In the wars; and that may you be bold to say in your foolery.

Feste: Well, God give them wisdom that have it, and those that are fools, let them use their talents.

Maria: Yet you will be hanged for being so long absent, or to be turned away, is not that as good as a hanging to you?

Feste: Many a good hanging prevents a bad marriage, and for turning away, let summer bear it out.

Maria: You are resolute, then?

Feste: Not so, neither, but I am resolved on two points.

Maria: That if one break, the other will hold, or if both break, your gaskins fall.

Feste: Apt, in good faith, very apt.

Well, go thy way if Sir Toby would leave drinking, thou wert as witty a piece of Eve's flesh as any in Illyria.

Maria: Peace, you rogue, no more of that.

Here comes my lady, make your excuse wisely, you were best.

(Exits)

Feste: Wit, and it be thy will, put me into good fooling!

Those wits, that think they have thee, do very often prove fools, and I, that I am, am sure I lack thee foolishness, that I may pass for a wise man.

For what says Quinapalus?

Better a witty fool, than a foolish wit.

(Olivia with Malvolio enter)

God bless thee, lady!

Olivia: Take the fool away.

Feste: Do you not hear, fellows? Take away the lady.

Olivia: Go to, you're a dry fool; I'll no more of you.

Besides, you grow dishonest.

Feste: Two faults, Madonna, that drink and good counsel will amend, for give the dry fool drink, then is the fool not dry.

Bid the dishonest man mend himself, if he mend, he is no longer dishonest.

If he cannot, let the botcher mend him.

Anything that's mended is but patched, virtue that transgresses is but patched with sin, and sin that amends is but patched with virtue.

If that this simple syllogism will serve, so if it will not, what is a remedy?

As there is no true cuckold but calamity, so beauty's a flower.

The lady bade take away the fool, therefore, I say again take her away.

Olivia: Sir, I bade them take away you.

Feste: Misprision in the highest degree! Lady, cucullus non facit monachum; that's as much to say as I wear not motley in my brain.

Good Madonna, give me leave to prove you a fool.

Olivia: Can you do it?

Feste: Dexterously, good Madonna.

Olivia: Make your proof.

Feste: I must catechise you for it, Madonna.

Good my mouse of virtue, answer me.

Olivia: Well, sir, for want of other idleness, I'll bide your proof.

Feste: Good Madonna, why mournest thou?

Olivia: Good fool, for my brother's death.

Feste: I think his soul is in hell, Madonna.

Olivia: I know his soul is in heaven, fool.

Feste: The more fool, Madonna, to mourn for your brother's soul being in heaven.

Take away the fool, gentlemen.

Olivia: What think you of this fool, Malvolio? Doth he not mend?

Malvolio: Yes, and shall do till the pangs of death shake him, infirmity, that decays the wise, doth ever make the better fool.

Feste: God send you, sir, a speedy infirmity for the better increasing your folly!

Sir Toby will be sworn that I am no fox, but he will not pass his word for two pence that you are no fool.

Olivia: How say you to that, Malvolio?

Malvolio: I marvel your ladyship takes delight in such a barren rascal.

I saw him put down the other day with an ordinary fool that has no more brain than a stone.

Look you now, he's out of his guard already, unless you laugh and minister occasion to him, he is gagged.

I protest, I take these wise men that crow so at these set kind of fools, no better than the fools' zanies.

Olivia: Oh, you are sick of self-love, Malvolio, and taste with a distempered appetite.

To be generous, guiltless and of free disposition, is to take those things for bird-bolts that you deem cannon-bullets.

There is no slander in an allowed fool, though he do nothing but rail, nor no railing in a known discreet man; though he do nothing but reprove.

Feste: Now Mercury endue thee with leasing, for thou speakest well of fools!

(Maria re-enters)

Maria: Madam, there is at the gate a young gentleman much desires to speak with you.

Olivia: From the Count Orsino, is it?

Maria: I know not, madam, it is a fair young man, and well attended.

Olivia: Who of my people hold him in delay?

Maria: Sir Toby, madam, your kinsman.

Olivia: Fetch him off, I pray you; he speaks nothing but madman: fie on him!

(Maria exits)

Go you Malvolio, if it be a suit from the count, I am sick, or not at home; what you will, to dismiss it.

(Malvolio exits)

Now you see, sir, how your fooling grows old and people dislike it.

Feste: Thou hast spoke for us, Madonna, as if thy eldest son should be a fool; whose skull Jove cram with brains!

For here he comes, one of thy kin has a most weak pia mater.

(Sir Toby Belch enters)

Olivia: By mine honour, half drunk. What is he at the gate, cousin?

Sir Toby Belch: A gentleman.

Olivia: A gentleman! What gentleman?

Sir Toby Belch: It is a gentle man here a plague of these pickle-herring!

How now, sot!

Feste: Good Sir Toby!

Olivia: Cousin, cousin, how have you come so early by this lethargy?

Sir Toby Belch: Lechery! I defy lechery. There's one at the gate.

Olivia: Ay, marry, what is he?

Sir Toby Belch: Let him be the devil, and he will, I care not.

Give me faith, say I.

Well, it's all one.

(Exits)

Olivia: What's a drunken man like, fool?

Feste: Like a drowned man, a fool and a mad man.

One draught above heat makes him a fool, the second mads him, and a third drowns him.

Olivia: Go thou and seek the crowner, and let him sit of my coz, for he's in the third degree of drink, he's drowned.

Go, look after him.

Feste: He is but mad yet, Madonna, and the fool shall look to the madman.

(Exits)

(Malvolio re-enters)

Malvolio: Madam, yond young fellow swears he will speak with you.

I told him you were sick, he takes on him to understand so much, and therefore comes to speak with you.

I told him you were asleep; he seems to have a foreknowledge of that too, and therefore comes to speak with you.

What is to be said to him, lady? He's fortified against any denial.

Olivia: Tell him he shall not speak with me.

Malvolio: Has been told so; and he says, he'll stand at your door like a sheriff's post, and be the supporter to a bench, but he'll speak with you.

Olivia: What kind of man is he?

Malvolio: Why, of mankind.

Olivia: What manner of man?

Malvolio: Of very ill manner; he'll speak with you, will you or no.

Olivia: Of what personage and years is he?

Malvolio: Not yet old enough for a man, nor young enough for a boy, as a squash is before it is a peascod, or a cooling when it is almost an apple.

It is with him in standing water, between boy and man.

He is very well-favoured and he speaks very shrewishly, one would think his mother's milk were scarce out of him.

Olivia: Let him approach: call in my gentlewoman.

Malvolio: Gentlewoman, my lady calls.

(Exits)

(Maria re-enters)

Olivia: Give me my veil, come, throw it over my face.

We'll once more hear Orsino's embassy.

(Viola, and Attendants enters)

Viola: The honourable lady of the house, which is she?

Olivia: Speak to me, I shall answer for her.

Your will?

Viola: Most radiant, exquisite and unmatchable beauty

I pray you, tell me if this be the lady of the house, for I never saw her.

I would be loath to cast away my speech, for besides that it is excellently well penned, I have taken great pains to coin it.

Good beauties, let me sustain no scorn, I am very compatible; even to the least sinister usage.

Olivia: Whence came you, sir?

Viola: I can say little more than I have studied, and that question's out of my part.

Good gentle one, give me modest assurance if you be the lady of the house, that I may proceed in my speech.

Olivia: Are you a comedian?

Viola: No, my profound heart: and yet, by the very fangs of malice I swear, I am not that I play.

Are you the lady of the house?

Olivia: If I do not usurp myself, I am.

Viola: Most certain, if you are she, you do usurp yourself, for what is yours to bestow is not yours to reserve, but this is from my commission.

I will on with my speech in your praise, and then show you the heart of my message.

Olivia: Come to what is important in it, I forgive you the praise.

Viola: Alas, I took great pains to study it, and it is poetical.

Olivia: It is the more like to be feigned.

I pray you, keep it in.

I heard you were saucy at my gates, and allowed your approach rather to wonder at you than to hear you.

If you be not mad, be gone; if you have reason and be brief.

It is not that time of moon with me to make one in so skipping a dialogue.

Maria: Will you hoist sail, sir? Here lies your way.

Viola: No, good swabber, I am to hull here a little longer.

Some mollification for your giant, sweet lady.

Tell me your mind, I am a messenger.

Olivia: Sure, you have some hideous matter to deliver, when the courtesy of it is so fearful.

Speak your office.

Viola: It alone concerns your ear.

I bring no overture of war, no taxation of homage.

I hold the olive in my hand, my words are as fun of peace as matter.

Olivia: Yet you began rudely. What are you? What would you?

Viola: The rudeness that hath appeared in me have I learned from my entertainment. What I am, and what I would, are as secret as maidenhead to your ears, divinity, to any other's, profanation.

Olivia: Give us the place alone: we will hear this divinity.

(Exeunt Maria and Attendants)

Now, sir, what is your text?

Viola: Most sweet lady.

Olivia: A comfortable doctrine, and much may be said of it.

Where lies your text?

Viola: In Orsino's bosom.

Olivia: In his bosom! In what chapter of his bosom?

Viola: To answer by the method, in the first of his heart.

Olivia: Oh I have read it: it is heresy. Have you no more to say?

Viola: Good madam, let me see your face.

Olivia: Have you any commission from your lord to negotiate with my face?

You are now out of your text, but we will draw the curtain and show you the picture.

Look you, sir, such a one I was this present, is it not well done?

(Unveiling)

Viola: Excellently done, if God did all.

Olivia: It is in grain, sir; it will endure wind and weather.

Viola: It is beauty truly blunt, whose red and white nature's own sweet and cunning hand laid on.

Lady, you are the cruell'st she alive, if you will lead these graces to the grave and leave the world no copy.

Olivia: Oh sir, I will not be so hard-hearted, I will give out divers schedules of my beauty. It shall be inventoried, and every particle and utensil labelled to my will.

As, item, two lips indifferent red, as item two grey eyes with lids to them, as item one neck, one chin, and so forth.

Were you sent hither to praise me?

Viola: I see you what you are, you are too proud, but if you were the devil, you are fair.

My lord and master loves you, oh such love could be but recompensed; though you were crowned

The nonpareil of beauty!

Olivia: How does he love me?

Viola: With adorations, fertile tears, with groans that thunder love, with sighs of fire.

Olivia: Your lord does know my mind, I cannot love him.

Yet I suppose him virtuous, know him noble, of great estate, of fresh and stainless youth; in voices well divulged, free, learned and valiant.

In dimension, and the shape of nature a gracious person, but yet I cannot love him; he might have took his answer long ago.

Viola: If I did love you in my master's flame, with such a suffering, such a deadly life.

In your denial I would find no sense, I would not understand it.

Olivia: Why, what would you?

Viola: Make me a willow cabin at your gate, and call upon my soul within the house; write loyal cantons of contemned love and sing them loud even in the dead of night.

Halloo your name to the reverberate hills, and make the babbling gossip of the air, cry out Olivia! Oh.

You should not rest between the elements of air and earth, but you should pity me!

Olivia: You might do much.

What is your parentage?

Viola: Above my fortunes, yet my state is well, I am a gentleman.

Olivia: Get you to your lord, I cannot love him; let him send no more unless perchance, you come to me again to tell me how he takes it.

Fare you well, I thank you for your pains: spend this for me.

Viola: I am no fee'd post lady, keep your purse; my master.

Not myself, lacks recompense, love make his heart of flint that you shall love, and let your fervor, like my master's, be placed in contempt!

Farewell, fair cruelty.

(Exits)

Olivia: 'What is your parentage?'

Above my fortunes, yet my state is well, I am a gentleman.

I'll be sworn thou art, thy tongue, thy face, thy limbs, actions and spirit do give thee five-fold blazon.

Not too fast, soft, soft!

Unless the master were the man. How now! Even so quickly may one catch the plague?

Methinks I feel this youth's perfections with an invisible and subtle stealth to creep in at mine eyes.

Well, let it be.

What oh, Malvolio!

(Malvolio re-enters)

Malvolio: Here, madam, at your service.

Olivia: Run after that same peevish messenger, the county's man: he left this ring behind him; would I or not tell him I'll none of it.

Desire him not to flatter with his lord, nor hold him up with hopes, I am not for him.

If that the youth will come this way to-morrow, I'll give him reasons for it, quicken thee Malvolio.

Malvolio: Madam, I will.

(Exits)

Olivia: I do I know not what, and fear to find mine eye too great a flatterer for my mind.

Fate, show thy force: ourselves we do not owe what is decreed must be, and be this so.

(Exits)

Act II, Scene 1

The sea-coast.

(Antonio and Sebastian enter)

Antonio: Will you stay no longer? Nor will you not that I go with you?

Sebastian: By your patience, no, my stars shine darkly over me.

The malignancy of my fate might perhaps distemper yours, therefore I shall crave of you your leave, that I may bear my evils alone.

It were a bad recompense for your love, to lay any of them on you.

Sebastian: No sooth sir, my determinate voyage is mere extravagancy, but I perceive in you so excellent a touch of modesty; that you will not extort from me what I am willing to keep in, therefore it charges me in manners the rather to express myself.

You must know of me then, Antonio, my name is Sebastian, which I called Roderigo.

My father was that Sebastian of Messaline, whom I know you have heard of.

He left behind him myself and a sister, both born in an hour: if the heavens had been pleased, would we had so ended! But you, sir, altered that for some hour before you took me from the breach of the sea was my sister drowned.

Antonio: Alas the day!

Sebastian: A lady, sir, though it was said she much resembled me, was yet of many accounted beautiful; but though I could not with such estimable wonder overfar believe that, yet thus far I will boldly publish her; she bore a mind that envy could not but call fair.

She is drowned already, sir, with salt water; though I seem to drown her remembrance again with more.

Antonio: Pardon me, sir, your bad entertainment.

Sebastian: Oh good Antonio, forgive me your trouble.

Antonio: If you will not murder me for my love, let me be your servant.

Sebastian: If you will not undo what you have done, that is, kill him whom you have recovered, desire it not.

Fare ye well at once: my bosom is full of kindness, and I am yet so near the manners of my mother; that upon the least occasion more mine eyes will tell tales of me.

I am bound to the Count Orsino's court, farewell.

(Exits)

Antonio: The gentleness of all the gods go with thee!

I have many enemies in Orsino's court, else would I very shortly see thee there, but come what may, I do adore thee so.

That danger shall seem sport, and I will go.

(Exits)

Act II, Scene 2

A street.

(Viola enters Malvolio following)

Malvolio: Were not you even now with the Countess Olivia?

Viola: Even now, sir; on a moderate pace I have since arrived but hither.

Malvolio: She returns this ring to you, sir, you might have saved me my pains; to have taken it away yourself.

She adds, moreover, that you should put your lord into a desperate assurance she will none of him; and one thing more, that you be never so hardy to come again in his affairs, unless it be to report your lord's taking of this.

Receive it so.

Viola: She took the ring of me, I'll none of it.

Malvolio: Come, sir, you peevishly threw it to her; and her will is, it should be so returned; if it be worth stooping for, there it lies in your eye, if not, be it his that finds it.

(Exits)

Viola: I left no ring with her: what means this lady?

Fortune forbid my outside have not charmed her!

She made good view of me; indeed, so much, that sure methought her eyes had lost her tongue, for she did speak in starts distractedly.

She loves me, sure, the cunning of her passion invites me in this churlish messenger.

None of my lord's ring! Why, he sent her none.

I am the man, if it be so, as it is.

Poor lady, she were better love a dream, disguise I see, thou art a wickedness wherein the pregnant enemy does much.

How easy is it for the proper-false in women's waxen hearts to set their forms!

Alas, our frailty is the cause, not we!

For such as we are made of, such we be.

How will this fadge? My master loves her dearly and I, poor monster, fond as much on him; and she mistaken, seems to dote on me.

What will become of this? As I am man, my state is desperate for my master's love, as I am woman; now alas the day!

What thriftless sighs shall poor Olivia breathe!

Oh time! Thou must untangle this, not I, it is too hard a knot for me to untie!

(Exits)

Act II, Scene 3

Olivia's house.

(Sir Toby Belch and Sir Andrew enter)

Sir Toby Belch: Approach, Sir Andrew: not to be abed after midnight is to be up betimes; and diluculo surgere, thou know'st.

Sir Andrew Aguecheek: Nay, my troth, I know not but I know; to be up late is to be up late.

Sir Toby Belch: A false conclusion, I hate it as an unfilled can to be up after midnight and to go to bed then, it is early.

So that to go to bed after midnight is to go to bed betimes.

Does not our life consist of the four elements?

Sir Andrew Aguecheek: Faith, so they say, but I think it rather consists of eating and drinking.

Sir Toby Belch: Thou'rt a scholar, let us therefore eat and drink.

Marian, I say! A stoup of wine!

(Jester enters)

Sir Andrew Aguecheek: Here comes the fool, in faith.

Feste: How now, my hearts! Did you never see the picture of we three?

Sir Toby Belch: Welcome ass. Now let's have a catch.

Sir Andrew Aguecheek: By my troth, the fool has an excellent breast.

I had rather than forty shillings I had such a leg, and so sweet a breath to sing, as the fool has.

In sooth, thou wast in very gracious fooling last night, when thou spokest of Pigrogromitus, of the Vapians passing the equinoctial of Queubus.

It was very good, In faith.

I sent thee sixpence for thy leman, hadst it?

Feste: I did impeticos thy gratillity, for Malvolio's nose is no whipstock, my lady has a white hand, and the Myrmidons are no bottle-ale houses.

Sir Andrew Aguecheek: Excellent! Why, this is the best fooling, when all is done.

Now, a song.

Sir Toby Belch: Come on, there is sixpence for you, let's have a song.

Sir Andrew Aguecheek: There's a testril of me too: if one knight give a…

Feste: Would you have a love-song, or a song of good life?

Sir Toby Belch: A love-song, a love-song.

Sir Andrew Aguecheek: Ay, ay, I care not for good life.

Feste: (Sings)

Oh mistress mine, where are you roaming?

Oh stay and hear; your true love's coming, that can sing both high and low.

Trip no further, pretty sweeting, journeys end in lovers meeting; every wise man's son doth know.

Sir Andrew Aguecheek: Excellent good, in faith.

Sir Toby Belch: Good, good.

Feste: (Sings)

What is love? It is not hereafter; present mirth hath present laughter.

What's to come is still unsure, in delay there lies no plenty, then come kiss me, sweet and twenty; youth's a stuff will not endure.

Sir Andrew Aguecheek: A mellifluous voice, as I am true knight.

Sir Toby Belch: A contagious breath.

Sir Andrew Aguecheek: Very sweet and contagious, in faith.

Sir Toby Belch: To hear by the nose, it is dulcet in contagion, but shall we make the welkin dance indeed? Shall we rouse the night-owl in a catch that will draw three souls out of one weaver? Shall we do that?

Sir Andrew Aguecheek: And you love me, let's do it, I am dog at a catch.

Feste: By'r lady, sir, and some dogs will catch well.

Sir Andrew Aguecheek: Most certain.

Let our catch be, Thou knave.

Feste: 'Hold thy peace, thou knave, knight? I shall be constrained in it to call thee knave, knight.

Sir Andrew Aguecheek: It is not the first time I have constrained one to call me knave.

Begin fool, it begins Hold thy peace.

Feste: I shall never begin if I hold my peace.

Sir Andrew Aguecheek: Good in faith.

Come, begin.

(Catch sung)

(Maria enters)

Maria: What a caterwauling do you keep here! If my lady have not called up her steward Malvolio and bid him turn you out of doors, never trust me.

Sir Toby Belch: My lady's a Cataian, we are politicians, Malvolio's a Peg-a-Ramsey, and Three merry men be we.

Am not I consanguineous? Am I not of her blood?

Tillyvally. Lady!

(Sings)

There dwelt a man in Babylon, lady, lady!

Feste: Beshrew me, the knight's in admirable fooling.

Sir Andrew Aguecheek: Ay, he does well enough if he be disposed, and so do I too, he does it with a better grace, but I do it more natural.

Sir Toby Belch: (Sings) Oh the twelfth day of December.

Maria: For the love of God, peace!

(Malvolio enters)

Malvolio: My masters, are you mad? or what are you? Have ye no wit, manners, nor honesty, but to gabble like tinkers at this time of night?

Do ye make an alehouse of my lady's house, that ye squeak out your coziers' catches without any mitigation or remorse of voice?

Is there no respect of place, persons, nor time in you?

Sir Toby Belch: We did keep time, sir, in our catches. Sneck up!

Malvolio: Sir Toby, I must be round with you.

My lady bade me tell you, that, though she harbours you as her kinsman, she's nothing allied to your disorders.

If you can separate yourself and your misdemeanors, you are welcome to the house; if not, and it would please you to take leave of her, she is very willing to bid you farewell.

Sir Toby Belch: 'Farewell, dear heart, since I must needs be gone.

Maria: Nay, good Sir Toby.

Feste: His eyes do show his days are almost done.

Malvolio: Is it even so?

Sir Toby Belch: But I will never die.

Feste: Sir Toby, there you lie.

Malvolio: This is much credit to you.

Sir Toby Belch: Shall I bid him go?

Feste: What and if you do?

Sir Toby Belch: Shall I bid him go, and spare not?

Feste: Oh no, no, no, no, you dare not.

Sir Toby Belch: Out of tune, sir, ye lie.

Art any more than a steward?

Dost thou think, because thou art virtuous, there shall be no more cakes and ale?

Feste: Yes, by Saint Anne, and ginger shall be hot in the mouth too.

Sir Toby Belch: Thou'rt in the right. Go, sir, rub your chain with crumbs.

A stoup of wine, Maria!

Malvolio: Mistress Mary, if you prized my lady's favour at anything more than contempt, you would not give means for this uncivil rule.

She shall know of it, by this hand.

(Exits)

Maria: Go shake your ears.

Sir Andrew Aguecheek: It were as good a deed as to drink when a man's a-hungry, to challenge him the field, and then to break promise with him and make a fool of him.

Sir Toby Belch: Do it, knight: I'll write thee a challenge, or I'll deliver thy indignation to him by word of mouth.

Maria: Sweet Sir Toby, be patient for tonight: since the youth of the count's was today with thy lady, she is much out of quiet.

For Monsieur Malvolio, let me alone with him.

if I do not gull him into a nayword, and make him a common recreation, do not think I have wit enough to lie straight in my bed; I know I can do it.

Sir Toby Belch: Possess us, possess us, tell us something of him.

Maria: Marry, sir, sometimes he is a kind of puritan.

Sir Andrew Aguecheek: Oh if I thought that I would beat him like a dog!

Sir Toby Belch: What, for being a puritan? Thy exquisite reason, dear knight?

Sir Andrew Aguecheek: I have no exquisite reason for it, but I have reason good enough.

Maria: The devil a puritan that he is, or anything constantly, but a time-pleaser, an affectioned ass that cons state without book and utters it by great swarths.

The best persuaded of himself, so crammed, as he thinks, with excellencies, that it is his grounds of faith that all that look on him love him; and on that vice in him will my revenge find notable cause to work.

Sir Toby Belch: What wilt thou do?

Maria: I will drop in his way some obscure epistles of love, wherein, by the colour of his beard, the shape of his leg, the manner of his gait, the expressure of his eye, forehead, and complexion, he shall find himself most feelingly personated.

I can write very like my lady your niece: on a forgotten matter we can hardly make distinction of our hands.

Sir Toby Belch: Excellent! I smell a device.

Sir Andrew Aguecheek: I have it in my nose too.

Sir Toby Belch: He shall think, by the letters that thou wilt drop, that they come from my niece, and that she's in love with him.

Maria: My purpose is, indeed, a horse of that colour.

Sir Andrew Aguecheek: And your horse now would make him an ass.

Maria: Ass, I doubt not.

Sir Andrew Aguecheek: Oh, it will be admirable!

Maria: Sport royal, I warrant you: I know my physic will work with him.

I will plant you two, and let the fool make a third, where he shall find the letter.

Observe his construction of it, for this night, to bed and dream on the event.

Farewell.

(Exits)

Sir Toby Belch: Good night, Penthesilea.

Sir Andrew Aguecheek: Before me, she's a good wench.

Sir Toby Belch: She's a beagle, true-bred, and one that adores me, what of that?

Sir Andrew Aguecheek: I was adored once too.

Sir Toby Belch: Let's to bed, knight. Thou hadst need send for more money.

Sir Andrew Aguecheek: If I cannot recover your niece, I am a foul way out.

Sir Toby Belch: Send for money, knight: if thou hast her not in the end, call me cut. 885**Sir Andrew Aguecheek:** If I do not, never trust me, take it how you will.

Sir Toby Belch: Come, come, I'll go burn some sack, it is too late to go to bed now: come, knight; come, knight.

(Exeunt)

Act II, Scene 4

Duke Orsino's palace.

(Duke Orsino, Viola, Curio, and others enter)

Orsino: Give me some music.

Now, good morrow, friends.

Now, good Cesario, but that piece of song, that old and antique song we heard last night.

Methought it did relieve my passion much, more than light airs and recollected terms of these most brisk and giddy-paced times.

Come, but one verse.

Curio: He is not here, so please your lordship that should sing it.

Orsino: Who was it?

Curio: Feste, the jester, my lord; a fool that the lady Olivia's father took much delight in.

He is about the house.

Orsino: Seek him out, and play the tune the while.

(Curio exits, music plays)

Come hither boy, if ever thou shalt love, in the sweet pangs of it remember me.

For such as I am all true lovers are, unstaid and skittish in all motions else save in the constant image of the creature that is beloved.

How dost thou like this tune?

Viola: It gives a very echo to the seat where Love is throned.

Orsino: Thou dost speak masterly:

My life upon it, young though thou art, thine eye hath stayed upon some favour that it loves:

Hath it not, boy?

Viola: A little, by your favour.

Orsino: What kind of woman is it?

Viola: Of your complexion.

Orsino: She is not worth thee, then.

What years, in faith?

Viola: About your years, my lord.

Orsino: Too old by heaven: let still the woman take an elder than herself so wears she to him; so sways she level in her husband's heart.

For boy, however we do praise ourselves, our fancies are more giddy and unfirm, more longing, wavering, sooner lost and worn, than women's are.

Viola: I think it well, my lord.

Orsino: Then let thy love be younger than thyself, or thy affection cannot hold the bent.

For women are as roses, whose fair flower being once displayed, doth fall that very hour.

Viola: And so they are: alas, that they are so; to die, even when they to perfection grow!

(Curio and Jester enter)

Orsino: Oh fellow come, the song we had last night.

Mark it, Cesario, it is old and plain; the spinsters and the knitters in the sun, and the free maids that weave their thread with bones.

Do use to chant it: it is silly sooth, and dallies with the innocence of love like the old age.

Feste: Are you ready, sir?

Orsino: Ay; pray to thee, sing.

(Music)

(Song)

Feste: Come away, come away, death, and in sad cypress let me be laid.

Fly away, fly away breath, I am slain by a fair cruel maid.

My shroud of white, stuck all with yew, oh prepare it!

My part of death, no one so true did share it.

Not a flower, not a flower sweet on my black coffin let there be strown; not a friend, not a friend greet, my poor corpse where my bones shall be thrown.

A thousand thousand sighs to save, lay me, Oh where sad true lover never find my grave, to weep there!

Orsino: There's for thy pains.

Feste: No pains, sir: I take pleasure in singing, sir.

Orsino: I'll pay thy pleasure then.

Feste: Truly, sir, and pleasure will be paid, one time or another.

Orsino: Give me now leave to leave thee.

Feste: Now, the melancholy god protect thee, and the tailor make thy doublet of changeable taffeta, for thy mind is a very opal.

I would have men of such constancy put to sea, that their business might be everything and their intent everywhere; for that's it that always makes a good voyage of nothing.

Farewell.

(Exits)

Orsino: Let all the rest give place.

(Curio and Attendants retire)

Once more, Cesario, get thee to yond same sovereign cruelty.

Tell her, my love, more noble than the world prizes not quantity of dirty lands.

The parts that fortune hath bestowed upon her, tell her I hold as giddily as fortune; but it is that miracle and queen of gems that nature pranks her in attracts my soul.

Viola: But if she cannot love you, sir?

Orsino: I cannot be so answered.

Viola: Sooth, but you must.

Say that some lady, as perhaps there is, hath for your love a great a pang of heart as you have for Olivia.

You cannot love her, you tell her so; must she not then be answered?

Orsino: There is no woman's sides can bide the beating of so strong a passion as love doth give my heart; no woman's heart so big, to hold so much, they lack retention.

Alas, their love may be called appetite, no motion of the liver, but the palate that suffer surfeit, cloyment and revolt; but mine is all as hungry as the sea, and can digest as much.

Make no compare between that love a woman can bear me and that I owe Olivia.

Viola: Ay, but I know.

Orsino: What dost thou know?

Viola: Too well what love women to men may owe.

In faith, they are as true of heart as we.

My father had a daughter loved a man, as it might be, perhaps, were I a woman, I should your lordship.

Orsino: And what's her history?

Viola: A blank, my lord. She never told her love, but let concealment, like a worm in the bud, feed on her damask cheek.

She pined in thought, and with a green and yellow melancholy she sat like patience on a monument, smiling at grief.

Was not this love indeed? We men may say more, swear more, but indeed our shows are more than will, for still we prove much in our vows; but little in our love.

Orsino: But died thy sister of her love, my boy?

Viola: I am all the daughters of my father's house, and all the brothers too, and yet I know not.

Sir, shall I to this lady?

Orsino: Ay, that's the theme.

To her in haste give her this jewel, say my love can give no place, bide no denay.

(Exeunt)

Act II, Scene 5

Olivia's garden.

(Sir Toby Belch, Sir Andrew, and Fabian enter)

Sir Toby Belch: Come thy ways, Signior Fabian

Fabian: Nay, I'll come: if I lose a scruple of this sport, let me be boiled to death with melancholy.

Sir Toby Belch: Wouldst thou not be glad to have the niggardly rascally sheep-biter come by some notable shame?

Fabian: I would exult, man: you know, he brought me out of favour with my lady about a bear-baiting here.

Sir Toby Belch: To anger him we'll have the bear again, and we will fool him black and blue; shall we not, Sir Andrew?

Sir Andrew Aguecheek: And we do not, it is pity of our lives.

Sir Toby Belch: Here comes the little villain.

(Maria enters)

How now, my metal of India!

Maria: Get ye all three into the box-tree.

Malvolio's coming down this walk, he has been yonder in the sun practising behavior to his own shadow this half hour.

Observe him, for the love of mockery, for I know this letter will make a contemplative idiot of him.

Close in the name of jesting! Lie thou there

(Throws down a letter)

For here comes the trout that must be caught with tickling.

(Exits)

(Malvolio enter)

Malvolio: It is but fortune, all is fortune.

Maria once told me she did affect me: and I have heard herself come thus near, that, should she fancy, it should be one of my complexion.

Besides, she uses me with a more exalted respect than anyone else that follows her.

What should I think on it?

Sir Toby Belch: Here's an overweening rogue!

Fabian: Oh peace! Contemplation makes a rare turkey-cock of him. How he jets under his advanced plumes!

Sir Andrew Aguecheek: Slight, I could so beat the rogue!

Sir Toby Belch: Peace, I say.

Malvolio: To be Count Malvolio!

Sir Toby Belch: Ah, rogue!

Sir Andrew Aguecheek: Pistol him, pistol him.

Sir Toby Belch: Peace, peace!

Malvolio: There is example for it, the lady of the Strachy married the yeoman of the wardrobe.

Sir Andrew Aguecheek: Fie on him, Jezebel!

Fabian: Oh peace! Now he's deeply in: look how imagination blows him.

Malvolio: Having been three months married to her, sitting in my state.

Sir Toby Belch: Oh for a stone-bow, to hit him in the eye!

Malvolio: Calling my officers about me, in my branched velvet gown, having come from a day-bed, where I have left Olivia sleeping.

Sir Toby Belch: Fire and brimstone!

Fabian: Oh peace, peace!

Malvolio: And then to have the humour of state; and after a demure travel of regard, telling them I know my place as I would they should do theirs, to for my kinsman Toby.

Sir Toby Belch: Bolts and shackles!

Fabian: Oh peace, peace, peace! Now, now.

Malvolio: Seven of my people, with an obedient start, make out for him.

I frown the while, and perchance wind up watch, or play with my somewhat rich jewel.

Toby approaches, courtesies there to me.

Sir Toby Belch: Shall this fellow live?

Fabian: Though our silence be drawn from us with cars, yet peace.

Malvolio: I extend my hand to him thus, quenching my familiar smile with an austere regard of control.

Sir Toby Belch: And does not Toby take you a blow of the lips then?

Malvolio: Saying, Cousin Toby, my fortunes having cast me on your niece give me this prerogative of speech.

Sir Toby Belch: What, what?

Malvolio: You must amend your drunkenness.

Sir Toby Belch: Out, scab!

Fabian: Nay, patience, or we break the sinews of our plot.

Malvolio: Besides, you waste the treasure of your time with a foolish knight.

Sir Andrew Aguecheek: That's me, I warrant you.

Malvolio: One Sir Andrew.

Sir Andrew Aguecheek: I knew it was I, for many do call me fool.

Malvolio: What employment have we here?

(Taking up the letter)

Fabian: Now is the woodcock near the gin.

Sir Toby Belch: Oh peace! and the spirit of humour intimate reading aloud to him!

Malvolio: By my life, this is my lady's hand these be her very C's, her U's and her T's and thus makes she her great P's.

It is, in contempt of question, her hand.

Sir Andrew Aguecheek: Her C's, her U's and her T's: why that?

Malvolio: (Reads) To the unknown beloved, this, and my good wishes.

Her very phrases! By your leave, wax soft! And the impressure her Lucrece, with which she uses to seal; it is my lady.

To whom should this be?

Fabian: This wins him, liver and all.

Malvolio: (Reads)

Jupiter knows I love, but who? When lips do not move, no man must know.

No man must know. What follows? The numbers altered!

No man must know, if this should be thee, Malvolio?

Sir Toby Belch: Marry, hang thee, brock!

Malvolio: (Reads)

I may command where I adore, but silence like a Lucrece knife; with bloodless stroke my heart doth gore.

M, O, A, I, doth sway my life.

Fabian: A fustian riddle!

Sir Toby Belch: Excellent wench, say I.

Malvolio: M, O, A, I, doth sway my life.'Nay, but first, let me see, let me see, let me see.

Fabian: What dish of poison has she dressed him!

Sir Toby Belch: And with what wing the signals cheques at it!

Malvolio: I may command where I adore.'

Why, she may command me, I serve her, she is my lady.

Why, this is evident to any formal capacity, there is no obstruction in this, and the end what should that alphabetical position portend?

If I could make that resemble something in me, softly! M, O, A, I.

Sir Toby Belch: Oh, ay, make up that, he is now at a cold scent.

Fabian: Sowter will cry upon it for all this, though it be as rank as a fox.

Malvolio: M... Malvolio; M... Why that begins my name.

Fabian: Did not I say he would work it out? The cur is excellent at faults.

Malvolio: M... but then there is no consonancy in the sequel that suffers under probation

A should follow but oh does.

Fabian: And Oh shall end, I hope.

Sir Toby Belch: Ay, or I'll cudgel him, and make him cry oh!

Malvolio: And then I comes behind.

Fabian: Ay, an you had any eye behind you, you might see more detraction at your heels than fortunes before you.

Malvolio: M, O, A, I; this simulation is not as the former, and yet, to crush this a little, it would bow to me, for every one of these letters are in my name, soft! here follows prose.

(Reads)

If this fall into thy hand, revolve.

In my stars I am above thee, but be not afraid of greatness.

Some are born great, some achieve greatness, and some have greatness thrust upon them.

Thy Fates open their hands; let thy blood and spirit embrace them, and to inure thyself to what thou art like to be, cast thy humble slough and appear fresh.

Be opposite with a kinsman, surly with servants, let thy tongue tang arguments of state; put thyself into the trick of singularity.

She thus advises thee that sighs for thee.

Remember who commended thy yellow stockings, and wished to see thee ever cross-gartered.

I say, remember, go to, thou art made; if thou desirest to be so.

If not, let me see thee a steward still, the fellow of servants, and not worthy to touch fortune's fingers.

Farewell.

She that would alter services with thee, the fortunate unhappy.

Daylight and champaign discovers not more, this is open.

I will be proud, I will read politic authors, I will baffle Sir Toby, I will wash off gross acquaintance, I will be point-devise the very man.

I do not now fool myself, to let imagination jade me, for every reason excites to this, that my lady loves me.

She did commend my yellow stockings of late, she did praise my leg being cross-gartered; and in this she manifests herself to my love, and with a kind of injunction drives me to these habits of her liking.

I thank my stars I am happy.

I will be strange, stout, in yellow stockings, and cross-gartered, even with the swiftness of putting on.

Jove and my stars be praised! Here is yet a postscript.

(Reads)

Thou canst not choose but know who I am.

If thou entertainest my love, let it appear in thy smiling, thy smiles become thee well, therefore in my presence still smile; dear my sweet, I pray to thee.

Jupiter, I thank thee, I will smile, I will do everything that thou wilt have me.

(Exits)

Fabian: I will not give my part of this sport for a pension of thousands to be paid from the Sophy.

Sir Toby Belch: I could marry this wench for this device.

Sir Andrew Aguecheek: So could I too.

Sir Toby Belch: And ask no other dowry with her but such another jest.

SirAndrew Aguecheek: Nor I neither.

Fabian: Here comes my noble gull-catcher.

(Maria re-enters)

Sir Toby Belch: Wilt thou set thy foot of my neck?

Sir Andrew Aguecheek: Or of mine either?

Sir Toby Belch: Shall I play my freedom at traytrip, and become thy bond-slave?

Sir Andrew Aguecheek: In faith, or I either?

Sir Toby Belch: Why, thou hast put him in such a dream, that when the image of it leaves him he must run mad.

Maria: Nay, but say true, does it work upon him?

Sir Toby Belch: Like aqua-vitae with a midwife.

Maria: If you will then see the fruits of the sport; mark his first approach before my lady.

He will come to her in yellow stockings, and it is a colour she abhors, and cross-gartered, a fashion she detests, and he will smile upon her, which will now be so unsuitable to her disposition; being addicted to a melancholy as she is, that it cannot but turn him into a notable contempt.

If you will see it, follow me.

Sir Toby Belch: To the gates of Tartar, thou most excellent devil of wit!

Sir Andrew Aguecheek: I'll make one too.

(Exeunt)

Act III, Scene 1

Olivia's garden.

(Viola, and Jester enter with a tabour)

Viola: Save thee, friend, and thy music: dost thou live by thy tabour?

Feste: No sir, I live by the church.

Viola: Art thou a churchman?

Feste: No such matter, sir, I do live by the church; for I do live at my house, and my house doth stand by the church.

Viola: So thou mayst say, the king lies by a beggar, if a beggar dwell near him; or, the church stands by thy tabour, if thy tabour stand by the church.

Feste: You have said, sir. To see this age! A sentence is but a cheveril glove to a good wit: how quickly the wrong side may be turned outward!

Viola: Nay, that's certain; they that dally nicely with words may quickly make them wanton.

Feste: I would, therefore, my sister had had no name, sir.

Viola: Why, man?

Feste: Why, sir, her name's a word; and to dally with that word might make my sister wanton. But indeed words are very rascals since bonds disgraced them.

Viola: Thy reason, man?

Feste: Troth sir, I can yield you none without words; and words are grown so false, I am loath to prove reason with them.

Viola: I warrant thou art a merry fellow and carest for nothing.

Feste: Not so, sir, I do care for something; but in my conscience, sir, I do not care for you: if that be to care for nothing, sir, I would it would make you invisible.

Viola: Art not thou the Lady Olivia's fool?

Feste: No, indeed, sir; the Lady Olivia has no folly, she will keep no fool, sir, till she be married, and fools are as like husbands as pilchards are to herrings; the husband's the bigger, I am indeed not her fool, but her corrupter of words.

Viola: I saw thee late at the Count Orsino's.

Feste: Foolery, sir, does walk about the orb like the sun,

It shines every where. I would be sorry, sir, but the fool should be as oft with your master as with my mistress.

I think I saw your wisdom there.

Viola: Nay, an thou pass upon me, I'll no more with thee.

Hold, there's expenses for thee.

Feste: Now Jupiter, in his next commodity of hair, send thee a beard!

Viola: By my troth, I'll tell thee, I am almost sick for one.

(From Aside)

Though I would not have it grow on my chin.

Is thy lady within?

Feste: Would not a pair of these have bred, sir?

Viola: Yes, being kept together and put to use.

Feste: I would play Lord Pandarus of Phrygia, sir, to bring a Cressida to this Troilus.

Viola: I understand you, sir; it is well begged.

Feste: The matter, I hope, is not great sir, begging but a beggar.

Cressida was a beggar.

My lady is within, sir.

I will construe to them whence you come, who you are and what you would are out of my welkin, I might say element, but the word is over-worn.

(Exits)

Viola: This fellow is wise enough to play the fool, and to do that well craves a kind of wit.

He must observe their mood on whom he jests, the quality of persons, and the time, and like the haggard, cheque at every feather that comes before his eye.

This is a practise as full of labour as a wise man's art.

For folly that he wisely shows is fit, but wise men, folly-fallen, quite taint their wit.

(Sir Toby Belch, and Sir Andrew enter)

Sir Toby Belch: Save you, gentleman.

Viola: And you, sir.

Sir Andrew Aguecheek: God guard you, sir.

Viola: And you as well, your servant.

Sir Andrew Aguecheek: I hope sir, you are, and I am yours.

Sir Toby Belch: Will you encounter the house? My niece is desirous, you should enter if your trade be to her.

Viola: I am bound to your niece sir; I mean she is the list of my voyage.

Sir Toby Belch: Taste your legs, sir; put them to motion.

Viola: My legs do better understand me, sir, than I understand what you mean by bidding me taste my legs.

Sir Toby Belch: I mean, to go, sir, to enter.

Viola: I will answer you with gait and entrance, but we are prevented.

(Olivia and Maria enter)

Most excellent accomplished lady, the heavens rain odours on you!

Sir Andrew Aguecheek: That youth's a rare courtier, rain odours well.

Viola: My matter hath no voice to your own most pregnant and vouchsafed ear.

Sir Andrew Aguecheek: Odours, pregnant and vouchsafed.

I'll get them, all three, all ready.

Olivia: Let the garden door be shut, and leave me to my hearing.

(Exeunt Sir Toby Belch, Sir Andrew, and Maria)

Give me your hand, sir.

Viola: My duty, madam, and most humble service.

Olivia: What is your name?

Viola: Cesario is your servant's name, fair princess.

Olivia: My servant sir! It was never merry world since lowly feigning was called compliment.

You're servant to the Count Orsino, youth.

Viola: And he is yours, and his must needs be yours.

Your servant's servant is your servant, madam.

Olivia: For him, I think not on him: for his thoughts, would they were blanks rather than filled with me!

Viola: Madam, I come to whet your gentle thoughts on his behalf.

Olivia: Oh by your leave, I pray you, I bade you never speak again of him; but would you undertake another suit.

I had rather hear you to solicit that than music from the spheres.

Viola: Dear lady.

Olivia: Give me leave, beseech you.

I did send, after the last enchantment, you did here a ring in chase of you.

So did I abuse myself, my servant and, I fear me, you.

Under your hard construction must I sit, to force that on you, in a shameful cunning, which you knew none of yours.

What might you think? Have you not set mine honour at the stake and baited it with all the unmuzzled thoughts that tyrannous heart can think?

To one of your receiving enough is shown; a cypress, not a bosom hideth my heart, so let me hear you speak.

Viola: I pity you.

Olivia: That's a degree to love.

Viola: No, not a prize, for it is a vulgar proof that very often we pity enemies.

Olivia: Why, then, methinks it is time to smile again.

Oh world, how apt the poor are to be proud!

If one should be a prey, how much the better to fall before the lion than the wolf!

(Clock strikes)

The clock upbraids me with the waste of time.

Be not afraid, good youth, I will not have you, and yet when wit and youth is come to harvest; your were is alike to reap a proper man.

There lies your way, due west.

Viola: Then westward-ho! Grace and good disposition attend your ladyship!

You'll nothing, madam, to my lord by me?

Olivia: Stay, I pray to thee, tell me what thou thinkest of me.

Viola: That you do think you are not what you are.

Olivia: If I think so, I think the same of you.

Viola: Then think you right: I am not what I am.

Olivia: I would you were as I would have you be!

Viola: Would it be better, madam, than I am?

I wish it might, for now I am your fool.

Olivia: Oh what a deal of scorn looks beautiful

In the contempt and anger of his lip! A murderous guilt shows not itself more soon.

Than love that would seem hid, love's night is noon; Cesario, by the roses of the spring, by maidhood, honour, truth and everything, I love thee so that despite all thy pride, nor wit, nor reason, can my passion hide.

Do not extort thy reasons from this clause, for that I woo, thou therefore hast no cause, but rather reason thus with reason fetter; love sought is good, but given unsought better.

Viola: By innocence I swear, and by my youth I have one heart, one bosom and one truth, and that no woman has; nor never none shall mistress be of it, save I alone.

And so adieu, good madam, never more will I my master's tears to you deplore.

Olivia: Yet come again; for thou perhaps mayst move that heart, which now abhors, to like his love.

(Exeunt)

Act III, Scene 2

Olivia's house.

(Sir Toby Belch, Sir Andrew, and Fabian enter)

Sir Andrew Aguecheek: No, faith, I'll not stay a jot longer.

Sir Toby Belch: Thy reason, dear venom, give thy reason.

Fabian: You must needs yield your reason, Sir Andrew.

Sir Andrew Aguecheek: Marry, I saw your niece do more favours to the count's serving-man than ever she bestowed upon me; I saw it in the orchard.

Sir Toby Belch: Did she see thee the while, old boy? Tell me that.

Sir Andrew Aguecheek: As plain as I see you now.

Fabian: This was a great argument of love in her toward you.

Sir Andrew Aguecheek: 'Slight, will you make an ass of me?

Fabian: I will prove it legitimate, sir, upon the oaths of judgment and reason.

Sir Toby Belch: And they have been grand-jury-men since before Noah was a sailor.

Fabian: She did show favour to the youth in your sight only to exasperate you, to awake your dormouse valour, to put fire in your heart and brimstone in your liver.

You should then have accosted her; and with some excellent jests, fire-new from the mint, you should have banged the youth into dumbness; this was looked for at your hand, and this was balked.

The double gilt of this opportunity you let time wash off, and you are now sailed into the north of my lady's opinion; where you will hang like an icicle on a Dutchman's beard, unless you do redeem it by some laudable attempt either of valour or policy.

Sir Andrew Aguecheek: And it be any way, it must be with valour; for policy

I hate.

I had as life be a Brownist as a politician.

Sir Toby Belch: Why, then, build me thy fortunes upon the basis of valour.

Challenge me the count's youth to fight with him, hurt him in eleven places, my niece shall take note of it; and assure thyself, there is no love-broker in the world can more prevail in man's commendation with woman than report of valour.

Fabian: There is no way but this, Sir Andrew.

Sir Andrew Aguecheek: Will either of you bear me a challenge to him?

Sir Toby Belch: Go, write it in a martial hand; be curst and brief; it is no matter how witty, so it be eloquent and fun of invention; taunt him with the licence of ink.

If thou thou'st him some thrice, it shall not be amiss; and as many lies as will lie in thy sheet of paper, although the sheet were big enough for the bed of Ware in England, set them down, go about it, let there beg all enough in thy ink; though thou write with a goose-pen, no matter about it.

Sir Andrew Aguecheek: Where shall I find you?

Sir Toby Belch: We'll call thee at the cubiculo, go.

(Sir Andrew exists)

Fabian: This is a dear manikin to you, Sir Toby.

Sir Toby Belch: I have been dear to him, lad, some two thousand strong, or so.

Fabian: We shall have a rare letter from him: but you'll not deliver it?

Sir Toby Belch: Never trust me, then; and by all means stir on the youth to an answer.

I think oxen and wainropes cannot hale them together.

For Andrew, if he were opened, and you find so much blood in his liver as will clog the foot of a flea, I'll eat the rest of the anatomy.

Fabian: And his opposite, the youth, bears in his visage no great presage of cruelty.

(Maria enters)

Sir Toby Belch: Look, where the youngest wren of nine comes.

Maria: If you desire the spleen, and will laugh yourself into stitches, follow me.

Yond gull Malvolio is turned heathen, a very renegado; for there is no Christian that means to be saved by believing rightly, can ever believe such impossible passages of grossness.

He's in yellow stockings.

Sir Toby Belch: And cross-gartered?

Maria: Most villainously, like a pedant that keeps a school in the church.

I have dogged him, like his murderer.

He does obey every point of the letter that I dropped to betray him.

He does smile his face into more lines than is in the new map with the augmentation of the Indies.

You have not seen such a thing as this.

I can hardly forbear hurling things at him, I know my lady will strike him.

If she do, he'll smile and take it for a great favour.

Sir Toby Belch: Come, bring us, bring us where he is.

(Exeunt)

Act III, Scene 3

A street.

(Sebastian and Antonio enter)

Sebastian: I would not by my will have troubled you; But, since you make your pleasure of your pains, I will no further chide you.

Antonio: I could not stay behind you.

My desire is more sharp than filed steel, which did spur me forth; and not all is love to see you, though so much as might have drawn one to a longer voyage; but jealousy that might befall your travel.

Being skilless in these parts, which to a stranger, unguided and unfriended, often prove rough and unhospitable.

My willing love, the rather by these arguments of fear set forth in your pursuit.

Sebastian: My kind Antonio,

I can see no other answer make me content but thanks, and thanks, and ever thanks; and often good turns are shuffled off with such uncurrent pay were my worth, as is my conscience firm.

You should find better dealing.

What's to do?

Shall we go see the reliques of this town?

Antonio: To-morrow, sir: best first go see your lodging.

Sebastian: I am not weary, and 'tis long to night.

I pray you, let us satisfy our eyes with the memorials and the things of fame that do renown this city.

Antonio: Would you, would you pardon me; I do not without danger walk these streets.

Once, in a sea-fight, against the count his galleys I did some service; of such note indeed, that were I taken here, it would scarce be answered.

Sebastian: Belike you slew great number of his people.

Antonio: The offence is not of such a bloody nature; Albeit the quality of the time and quarrel might well have given us bloody argument.

It might have since been answered in repaying, what we took from them, which for traffic's sake most of our city did.

Only myself stood out, for which if I be lapsed in this place, I shall pay dear.

Sebastian: Do not then walk too open.

Antonio: It doth not fit me.

Hold, sir, here's my purse.

In the south suburbs, at the Elephant, is best to lodge.

I will bespeak our diet, whiles you beguile the time and feed your knowledge; with viewing of the town, there shall you have me.

Sebastian: Why I your purse?

Antonio: Happily your eye shall light upon some toy.

You have desire to purchase and suit your store, I think, is not for idle markets sir.

Sebastian: I'll be your purse-bearer and leave you for an hour.

Antonio: To the Elephant.

Sebastian: I do remember.

(Exeunt)

Act III, Scene 4

Olivia's garden.

(Olivia and Maria enter**)**

Olivia: I have sent after him, he says he'll come. How shall I feast him? What bestow of him?

For youth is bought more oft than begged or borrowed; I speak too loud.

Where is Malvolio? He is sad and civil, and suits well for a servant with my fortunes.

Where is Malvolio?

Maria: He's coming madam, but in very strange manner; he is sure possessed, madam.

Olivia: Why, what's the matter? Does he rave?

Maria: No madam, he does nothing but smile, your ladyship were best to have some guard about you if he come; for sure the man is tainted in's wits.

Olivia: Go call him hither.

(Maria exists)

I am as mad as he, if sad and merry madness equal be.

(Maria re-enters with Malvolio)

How now, Malvolio!

Malvolio: Sweet lady, oh, oh.

Olivia: Smilest thou? I sent for thee upon a sad occasion.

Malvolio: Sad, lady! I could be sad, this does make some obstruction in the blood.

This cross-gartering what of that?

If it please the eye of one, it is with me as the very true sonnet does please one and please all.

Olivia: Why, how dost thou, man? What is the matter with thee?

Malvolio: Not black in my mind, though yellow in my legs.

It did come to his hands, and commands shall be executed.

I think we do know the sweet Roman hand.

Olivia: Wilt thou go to bed, Malvolio?

Malvolio: To bed! Ay sweet-heart, and I'll come to thee.

Olivia: God comfort thee! Why dost thou smile so and kiss thy hand so oft?

Maria: How do you, Malvolio?

Malvolio: At your request! Yes, nightingales answer does.

Maria: Why appear you with this ridiculous boldness before my lady?

Malvolio: Be not afraid of greatness. It was well written.

Olivia: What meanest thou by that, Malvolio?

Malvolio: Some are born great.

Olivia: Ha!

Malvolio: Some achieve greatness.

Olivia: What sayest thou?

Malvolio: And some have greatness thrust upon them.

Olivia: Heaven restore thee!

Malvolio: Remember who commended thy yellow stockings.

Olivia: Thy yellow stockings!

Malvolio: And wished to see thee cross-gartered.

Olivia: Cross-gartered!

Malvolio: Go to thou art made, if thou desirest to be so.

Olivia: Am I made?

Malvolio: If not, let me see thee a servant still.

Olivia: Why, this is very midsummer madness.

(Servant enters)

Servant: Madam, the young gentleman of the Count Orsino's is returned.

I could hardly entreat him back, he attends your ladyship's pleasure.

Olivia: I'll come to him.

(Servant exits)

Good Maria, let this fellow be looked to.

Where's my cousin Toby? Let some of my people have a special care of him; I would not have him miscarry for the half of my dowry.

(Exeunt Olivia and Maria)

Malvolio: Oh oh! Do you come near me now? No worse man than Sir Toby to look to me! This concurs directly with the letter.

She sends him on purpose, that I may appear stubborn to him for she incites me to that in the letter.

Cast thy humble slough, says she, be opposite with a kinsman, surly with servants; let thy tongue tang with arguments of state, put thyself into the trick of singularity.

Consequently, set down the manner how, as a sad face, a reverend carriage, a slow tongue in the habit of some soar note, and so forth.

I have timed her; but it is Jupiter's doing, and Jupiter make me thankful! And when she went away now, let this fellow be looked to.

Fellow not Malvolio, nor after my degree, but fellow, why, everything adheres together that no dram of a scruple, no scruple of a scruple, no obstacle, no incredulous or unsafe circumstance; what can be said?

Nothing that can be can come between me and the full prospect of my hopes.

Well, Jupiter not I is the doer of this, and he is to be thanked.

(Maria re-enters with Sir Toby Belch and Fabian)

Sir Toby Belch: Which way is he, in the name of sanctity?

If all the devils of hell be drawn in little, and Legion himself possessed him, yet I'll speak to him.

Fabian: Here he is, here he is. How is it with you, sir? How is it with you man?

Malvolio: Go off, I discard you; let me enjoy my private.

Go off.

Maria: Lord, how hollow the fiend speaks within him! Did not I tell you?

Sir Toby, my lady prays you to have a care of him.

Malvolio: Ah, ha! does she so?

Sir Toby Belch: Go to, go to; peace, peace; we must deal gently with him.

Let me alone.

How do you, Malvolio? how is it with you? What, man!

Defy the devil, consider he's an enemy to mankind.

Malvolio: Do you know what you say?

Maria: La you, and you speak ill of the devil, how he takes it at heart! Pray God, he be not bewitched!

Fabian: Carry his water to the wise woman.

Maria: Marry, and it shall be done to-morrow morning, if I live.

My lady would not lose him for more than I'll say.

Malvolio: How now, mistress!

Maria: Oh Lord!

Sir Toby Belch: Pray to thee, hold thy peace, this is not the way.

Do you not see you move him? Let me alone with him.

Fabian: No way but gentleness; gently, gently.

The fiend is rough and will not be roughly used.

Sir Toby Belch: Why, how now, my bawcock! How dost thou, chuck?

Malvolio: Sir!

Sir Toby Belch: Ay, Biddy, come with me. What, man! It is not for gravity to play at cherry-pit with Satan; hang him, foul collier!

Maria: Get him to say his prayers, good Sir Toby, get him to pray.

Malvolio: My prayers, minx!

Maria: No, I warrant you, he will not hear of godliness.

Malvolio: Go, hang yourselves all! You are idle shallow things.

I am not of your element, you shall know more hereafter.

(Exits)

Sir Toby Belch: Is it possible?

Fabian: If this were played upon a stage now, I could condemn it as an improbable fiction.

Sir Toby Belch: His very genius hath taken the infection of the device, man.

Maria: Nay, pursue him now, lest the device take air and taint.

Fabian: Why, we shall make him mad indeed.

Maria: The house will be the quieter.

Sir Toby Belch: Come, we'll have him in a dark room and bound.

My niece is already in the belief that he's mad.

We may carry it thus, for our pleasure and his penance, till our very pastime, tired out of breath, prompt us to have mercy on him.

At which time we will bring the device to the bar and crown thee for a finder of madmen, but see, but see.

(Sir Andrew enter)

Fabian: More matter for a May morning.

Sir Andrew Aguecheek: Here's the challenge, read it, warrant there's vinegar and pepper in it.

Fabian: Is it so saucy?

Sir Andrew Aguecheek: Ay, is it, I warrant him: do but read.

Sir Toby Belch: Give me.

(Reads)

Youth, whatsoever thou art, thou art but a scurvy fellow.

Fabian: Good, and valiant.

Sir Toby Belch: (Reads) Wonder not, nor admire not in thy mind, why I do call thee so, for I will show thee no reason for it.

Fabian: A good note; that keeps you from the blow of the law.

Sir Toby Belch: (Reads) Thou comest to the lady Olivia, and in my sight she uses thee kindly, but thou liest in thy throat; that is not the matter I challenge thee for.

Fabian: Very brief, and to exceeding good senseless.

Sir Toby Belch: (Reads) I will waylay thee going home; where if it be thy chance to kill me.

Fabian: Good.

Sir Toby Belch: (Reads) Thou killest me like a rogue and a villain.

Fabian: Still you keep of the windy side of the law; good.

Sir Toby Belch: (Reads) Fare thee well; and God have mercy upon one of our souls! He may have mercy upon mine, but my hope is better, and so look to thyself.

Thy friend, as thou usest him, and thy sworn enemy, Andrew Aguecheek.

If this letter move him not, his legs cannot, I'll give it to him.

Maria: You may have very fit occasion for it, he is now in some commerce with my lady, and will by and by depart.

Sir Toby Belch: Go, Sir Andrew, scout me for him at the corner the orchard like a bum-baily; so soon as ever thou seest him, draw, and as thou drawest swear horrible for it comes to pass often that a terrible oath.

A swaggering accent sharply twanged of gives manhood more approbation than ever proof itself would have earned him.

Away!

Sir Andrew Aguecheek: Nay, let me alone for swearing.

(Exits)

Sir Toby Belch: Now will not I deliver his letter, for the behavior of the young gentleman gives him out to be of good capacity and breeding; his employment between his lord and my niece confirms no less, therefore this letter being so excellently ignorant, will breed no terror in the youth.

He will find it comes from a clodpole, but sir I will deliver his challenge by word of mouth; set upon Aguecheek a notable report of valour and drive the gentleman; as I know his youth will aptly receive it, into a most hideous opinion of his rage, skill, fury and impetuosity.

This will so fright them both that they will kill one another by the look, like cockatrices.

(Olivia re-enters with Viola)

Fabian: Here he comes with your niece; give them way till he take leave, and presently after him.

Sir Toby Belch: I will meditate the while upon some horrid message for a challenge.

(Exeunt Sir Toby Belch, Fabian, and Maria)

Olivia: I have said too much unto a heart of stone and laid mine honour too unchary out, there's something in me that reproves my fault, but such a headstrong potent fault it is; that it but mocks reproof.

Viola: With the same behavior that your passion bears goes on my master's grief.

Olivia: Here, wear this jewel for me, it is my picture, refuse it not, it hath no tongue to vex you; and I beseech you come again to-morrow.

What shall you ask of me that I'll deny, that honour saved may upon asking give?

Viola: Nothing but this; your true love for my master.

Olivia: How with mine honour may I give him that which I have given to you?

Viola: I will acquit you.

Olivia: Well, come again to-morrow, fare thee well.

A fiend like thee might bear my soul to hell.

(Exits)

(Sir Toby Belch and Fabian re-enter)

Sir Toby Belch: Gentleman, God save thee.

Viola: And you, sir.

Sir Toby Belch: That defence thou hast, betake thee to it, of what nature the wrongs are thou hast done him I know not; but thy intercepter, full of despite, bloody as the hunter, attends thee at the orchard-end.

Dismount thy tuck, be yare in thy preparation, for thy assailant is quick, skilful and deadly.

Viola: You mistake, sir; I am sure no man hath any quarrel to me, my remembrance is very free and clear from any image of offence done to any man.

Sir Toby Belch: You'll find it otherwise, I assure you, therefore if you hold your life at any price, betake you to your guard; for your opposite hath in him what youth, strength, skill and wrath can furnish man withal.

Viola: I pray you, sir, what is he?

Sir Toby Belch: He is knight, dubbed with unhatched sword and on carpet consideration, but he is a devil in private 1brawl; souls and bodies hath he divorced three, and his incensement at this moment is so implacable that satisfaction can be none but by pangs of death and sepulchre.

Hob, nob, is his word; give it or take it.

Viola: I will return again into the house and desire some conduct of the lady.

I am no fighter.

I have heard of some kind of men that put quarrels purposely on others, to taste their valour, belike this is a man of that quirk.

Sir Toby Belch: Sir, no, his indignation derives itself out of a very competent injury; therefore get you on and give him his desire.

Back you shall not to the house, unless you undertake that with me which with as much safety you might answer him, therefore, on, or strip your sword stark naked; for meddle you must that's certain, or forswear to wear iron about you.

Viola: This is as uncivil as strange. I beseech you, do me this courteous office, as to know of the knight what my offence to him is, it is something of my negligence, nothing of my purpose.

Sir Toby Belch: I will do so. Signior Fabian, stay you by this gentleman till my return.

(Exits)

Viola: Pray you, sir, do you know of this matter?

Fabian: I know the knight is incensed against you, even to a mortal arbitrement; but nothing of the circumstance more.

Viola: I beseech you, what manner of man is he?

Fabian: Nothing of that wonderful promise, to read him by his form, as you are like to find him in the proof of his valour.

He is, indeed, sir, the most skilful, bloody and fatal opposite that you could possibly have found in any part of Illyria.

Will you walk towards him?

I will make your peace with him if I can.

Viola: I shall be much bound to you for it: I am one that had rather go with sir priest than sir knight; I care not who knows so much of my mettle.

(Exeunt)

(Sir Toby Belch re-enters with Sir Andrew)

Sir Toby Belch: Why, man, he's a very devil; I have not seen such a firago.

I had a pass with him, sword, scabbard and all, and he gives me the stuck in with such a mortal motion, that it is inevitable; and on the answer he pays you as surely as your feet hit the ground they step on.

They say he has been fencer to the Sophy.

Sir Andrew Aguecheek: Pox on it, I'll not meddle with him.

Sir Toby Belch: Ay, but he will not now be pacified.

Fabian can scarce hold him yonder.

Sir Andrew Aguecheek: Plague on it, and I thought he had been valiant and so cunning in fence, I' would have seen him damned here I would have challenged him.

Let him let the matter slip, and I'll give him my horse, grey Capilet.

Sir Toby Belch: I'll make the motion: stand here, make a good show on it.

This shall end without the perdition of souls.

(From Aside)

Marry, I'll ride your horse as well as I ride you.

(Fabian and Viola re-enter)

(To Fabian)

I have his horse to take up the quarrel, I have persuaded him the youth's a devil.

Fabian: He is as horribly conceited of him; and pants and looks pale, as if a bear were at his heels.

Sir Toby Belch: (To Viola) There's no remedy, sir, he will fight with you for his oath sake.

Merrily, he hath better bethought him of his quarrel, and he finds that now scarce to be worth talking of: therefore draw, for the supportance of his vow, he protests, he will not hurt you.

Viola: (From Aside) Pray God defend me! A little thing would make me tell them how much I lack of a man.

Fabian: Give ground, if you see him furious.

Sir Toby Belch: Come, Sir Andrew, there's no remedy, the gentleman will for his honour's sake, have one bout with you; he cannot by the duello avoid it, but he has promised me as he is a gentleman and a soldier, he will not hurt you.

Come on, to it.

Sir Andrew Aguecheek: Pray God, he keep his oath!

Viola: I do assure you, 'tis against my will.

(They draw)

(Enter Antonio)

Antonio: Put up your sword. If this young gentleman have done offence, I take the fault on me; if you offend him, I for him defy you.

Sir Toby Belch: You, sir! Why, what are you?

Antonio: One, sir, that for his love dares yet do more

Than you have heard him brag to you he will.

Sir Toby Belch: Nay, if you be an undertaker, I am for you.

(They draw)

(Enter Officers)

Fabian: Oh good Sir Toby, Hold! Here come the officers.

Sir Toby Belch: I'll be with you anon.

Viola: Pray, sir, put your sword up, if you please.

Sir Andrew Aguecheek: Marry, will I, sir; and, for that I promised you, I'll be as good as my word; he will bear you easily and reins well.

First Officer: This is the man, do thy office.

Second Officer: Antonio, I arrest thee at the suit of Count Orsino.

Antonio: You do mistake me, sir.

First Officer: No, sir, no jot; I know your favour well, though now you have no sea-cap on your head.

Take him away, he knows I know him well.

Antonio: I must obey.

(To Viola)

This comes with seeking you, but there's no remedy; I shall answer it.

What will you do, now my necessity makes me to ask you for my purse?

It grieves me much more for what I cannot do for you than what befalls myself.

You stand amazed, but be of comfort.

Second Officer: Come, sir, away.

Antonio: I must entreat of you some of that money.

Viola: What money, sir?

For the fair kindness you have showed me here, and in part being prompted by your present trouble, out of my lean and low ability I'll lend you something.

My having is not much, I'll make division of my present with you; hold, there's half my coffer.

Antonio: Will you deny me now?

Is it possible that my deserts to you can lack persuasion?

Do not tempt my misery, lest that it make me so unsound a man as to upbraid you with those kindnesses that I have done for you.

Viola: I know of none; nor know I you by voice or any feature.

I hate ingratitude more in a man than lying, vainness, babbling, drunkenness, or any taint of vice whose strong corruption inhabits our frail blood.

Antonio: Oh heavens themselves!

Second Officer: Come, sir, I pray you, go.

Antonio: Let me speak a little.

This youth that you see here I snatched one half out of the jaws of death, relieved him with such sanctity of love, and to his image which methought did promise most venerable worth, did I devotion.

First Officer: What's that to us? The time goes by, away!

Antonio: But oh how vile an idol proves this god, thou hast, Sebastian, done good feature shame.

In nature there's no blemish but the mind, none can be called deformed but the unkind.

Virtue is beauty, but the beauteous evil are empty trunks overflourished by the devil.

First Officer: The man grows mad, away with him! Come, come, sir.

Antonio: Lead me on.

(Officers exits)

Viola: Methinks his words do from such passion fly, that he believes himself.

So do not I, prove true imagination, oh prove true, that I dear brother, be now taken for you!

Sir Toby Belch: Come hither, knight; come hither, Fabian.

We'll whisper o'er a couplet or two of most sage saws.

Viola: He named Sebastian, I my brother know, yet living in my glass; even such and so in favour was my brother, and he went still in this fashion, colour, ornament, for him I imitate.

Oh if it prove, Tempests are kind and salt waves fresh in love.

(Exits)

Sir Toby Belch: A very dishonest paltry boy, and more a coward than a hare, his dishonesty appears in leaving his friend here in necessity and denying him; and for his cowardship, ask Fabian.

Fabian: A coward, a most devout coward, religious in it.

Sir Andrew Aguecheek: Slid, I'll after him again and beat him.

Sir Toby Belch: Do, cuff him soundly, but never draw thy sword.

Sir Andrew Aguecheek: An I do not.

Fabian: Come, let's see the event.

Sir Toby Belch: I dare lay any money it will be nothing yet.

(Exeunt)

Act IV, Scene 1

Before Olivia's house.

(Sebastian and Jester enter)

Feste: Will you make me believe that I am not sent for you?

Sebastian: Go to, go to, thou art a foolish fellow.

Let me be clear of thee.

Feste: Well held out, in faith! No, I do not know you; nor I am not sent to you by my lady, to bid you come speak with her, nor your name is not Master Cesario, nor this is not my nose neither.

Nothing that is so is so.

Sebastian: I pray to thee, vent thy folly somewhere else.

Thou know'st not me.

Feste: Vent my folly! He has heard that word of some great man and now applies it to a fool.

Vent my folly!

I am afraid this great lubber, the world will prove a cockney.

I pray to thee now, ungird thy strangeness and tell me what I shall vent to my lady.

Shall I vent to her that thou art coming?

Sebastian: I pray to thee, foolish Greek, depart from me.

There's money for thee, if you tarry longer, I shall give worse payment.

Feste: By my troth, thou hast an open hand, these wise men that give fools money get themselves a good report, after fourteen years' purchase.

(Sir Andrew, Sir Toby Belch, and Fabian enter)

Sir Andrew Aguecheek: Now, sir, have I met you again? there's for you.

Sebastian: Why, there's for thee, and there, and there.

Are all the people mad?

Sir Toby Belch: Hold, sir, or I'll throw your dagger over the house.

Feste: This will I tell my lady straight: I would not be in some of your coats for two pence.

(Exits)

Sir Toby Belch: Come on, sir, hold.

Sir Andrew Aguecheek: Nay, let him alone, I'll go another way to work with him; I'll have an action of battery against him, if there be any law in Illyria.

Though I struck him first, yet it's no matter for that.

Sebastian: Let go thy hand.

Sir Toby Belch: Come, sir, I will not let you go.

Come, my young soldier, put up your iron.

You are well fleshed; come on.

Sebastian: I will be free from thee.

What wouldst thou now? If thou darest tempt me further, draw thy sword.

Sir Toby Belch: What, what? Nay, then I must have an ounce or two of this malapert blood from you.

(Olivia enters)

Olivia: Hold, Toby; on thy life I charge thee, hold!

Sir Toby Belch: Madam!

Olivia: Will it be ever thus? Ungracious wretch, fit for the mountains and the barbarous caves, where manners never were preached! Out of my sight!

Be not offended, dear Cesario.

Rudesby, be gone!

(Exeunt Sir Toby Belch, Sir Andrew, and Fabian)

I pray to thee, gentle friend, let thy fair wisdom, not thy passion, sway in this uncivil and thou unjust extent against thy peace.

Go with me to my house, and hear thou there how many fruitless pranks this ruffian hath botched up, that thou thereby mayst smile at this, thou shalt not choose but go.

Do not deny.

Beshrew his soul for me, he started one poor heart of mine in thee.

Sebastian: What relish is in this? How runs the stream?

Or I am mad, or else this is a dream, let fancy still my sense in Lethe steep; if it be thus to dream, still let me sleep!

Olivia: Nay, come, I pray to thee; would thou'ldst be ruled by me!

Sebastian: Madam, I will.

Olivia: Oh say so, And so be!

(Exeunt)

Act IV, Scene 2

Olivia's house.

(Maria and Jester enter)

Maria: Nay, I pray to thee, put on this gown and this beard, make him believe thou art Sir Topas the curate.

Do it quickly, I'll call Sir Toby the whilst.

(Exits)

Feste: Well, I'll put it on, and I will dissemble myself in it, and I would I were the first that ever dissembled in such a gown.

I am not tall enough to become the function well, nor lean enough to be thought a good student; but to be said an honest man and a good housekeeper goes as fairly as to say a careful man and a great scholar.

The competitors enter.

(Sir Toby Belch and Maria enter)

Sir Toby Belch: Jove bless thee, master Parson.

Feste: Bonos dies, Sir Toby: for, as the old hermit of Prague, that never saw pen and ink, very wittily said to a niece of King Gorboduc: That that is is; so I being Master Parson, am Master Parson, for what is that, but that, and is but is?

Sir Toby Belch: To him, Sir Topas.

Feste: What, ho, I say! peace in this prison!

Sir Toby Belch: The knave counterfeits well; a good knave.

Malvolio: (Within) Who calls there?

Feste: Sir Topas the curate, who comes to visit Malvolio the lunatic.

Malvolio: Sir Topas, Sir Topas, good Sir Topas, go to my lady.

Feste: Out, hyperbolical fiend! How vexest thou this man!

Talkest thou nothing but of ladies?

Sir Toby Belch: Well said, Master Parson.

Malvolio: Sir Topas, never was man thus wronged.

Good Sir Topas, do not think I am mad: they have laid me here in hideous darkness.

Feste: Fie, thou dishonest Satan! I call thee by the most modest terms, for I am one of those gentle ones that will use the devil himself with courtesy.

Sayest thou that house is dark?

Malvolio: As hell, Sir Topas.

Feste: Why it hath bay windows transparent as barricadoes, and the clearstores toward the south north are as lustrous as ebony; and yet complainest thou of obstruction?

Malvolio: I am not mad, Sir Topas: I say to you, this house is dark.

Feste: Madman, thou errest, I say, there is no darkness but ignorance, in which thou art more puzzled than the Egyptians in their fog.

Malvolio: I say this house is as dark as ignorance, though ignorance were as dark as hell; and I say there was never man thus abused.

I am no more mad than you are, make the trial of it in any constant question.

Feste: What is the opinion of Pythagoras concerning wild fowl?

Malvolio: That the soul of our grandam might haply inhabit a bird.

Feste: What thinkest thou of his opinion?

Malvolio: I think nobly of the soul, and no way approve his opinion.

Feste: Fare thee well. Remain thou still in darkness, thou shalt hold the opinion of Pythagoras were I will allow of thy wits, and fear to kill a woodcock, lest thou dispossess the soul of thy grandam.

Fare thee well.

Malvolio: Sir Topas, Sir Topas!

Sir Toby Belch: My most exquisite Sir Topas!

Feste: Nay, I am for all waters.

Maria: Thou mightst have done this without thy beard and gown; he sees thee not.

Sir Toby Belch: To him in thine own voice, and bring me word how thou findest him, I would we were well rid of this knavery.

If he may be conveniently delivered, I would he were, for I am now so far in offence with my niece that I cannot pursue with any safety this sport to the upshot.

Come by and by to my chamber.

(Exeunt Sir Toby Belch and Maria)

Feste: (Singing)

Hey Robin, oh jolly Robin; tell me how thy lady does.

Malvolio: Fool!

Feste: My lady is unkind, perdy.

Malvolio: Fool!

Feste: Alas, why is she so?

Malvolio: Fool, I say!

Feste: She loves another, who calls, ha?

Malvolio: Good fool, as ever thou wilt deserve well at my hand, help me to a candle, and pen, ink and paper.

As I am a gentleman, I will live to be thankful to thee for it.

Feste: Master Malvolio?

Malvolio: Ay, good fool.

Feste: Alas, sir, how fell you besides your five wits?

Malvolio: Fool, there was never a man so notoriously abused, I am as well in my wits, fool, as thou art.

Feste: But as well? Then you are mad indeed, if you be no better in your wits than a fool.

Malvolio: They have here propertied me; keep me in darkness, send ministers to me, asses, and do all they can to face me out of my wits.

Feste: Advise you what you say, the minister is here.

Malvolio, Malvolio, thy wits the heavens restore!

Endeavour thyself to sleep, and leave thy vain bibble babble.

Malvolio: Sir Topas!

Feste: Maintain no words with him, good fellow.

Who I, sir? Not I sir. God be willing, you good Sir Topas.

Merry, amen. I will, sir, I will.

Malvolio: Fool, fool, fool, I say!

Feste: Alas, sir, be patient. What say you sir? I am shent for speaking to you.

Malvolio: Good fool, help me to some light and some paper, I tell thee I am as well in my wits as any man in Illyria.

Feste: Well-a-day that you were, sir.

Malvolio: By this hand, I am.

Good fool, some ink, paper and light, and convey what I will set down to my lady, it shall advantage thee more than ever the bearing of letter did.

Feste: I will help you to it. But tell me true, are you not mad indeed?

Or do you but counterfeit?

Malvolio: Believe me, I am not; I tell thee true.

Feste: Nay, I'll ne'er believe a madman till I see his brains.

I will fetch you light and paper and ink.

Malvolio: Fool, I'll requite it in the highest degree, pray to thee, be gone.

Feste: (Singing)

I am gone, sir, and anon sir.

I'll be with you again, as a trice.

Like to the old Vice, your need to sustain.

Who, with dagger of lath, in his rage and his wrath, cries, ah, ha!

To the devil, like a mad lad, prepare thy nails, dad.

Adieu, good man devil.

(Exits)

Act IV, Scene 3

Olivia's garden.

(Sebastian enter)

Sebastian: This is the air, that is the glorious sun, this pearl she gave me.

I do feel it and see it, and though it is wonder that enwraps me thus, yet it is not madness.

Where's Antonio, then? I could not find him at the Elephant.

Yet there he was; and there I found this credit, that he did range the town to seek me out.

His counsel now might do me golden service, for though my soul disputes well with my sense that this may be some error, but no madness.

Yet doth this accident and flood of fortune so far exceed all instance, all discourse, that I am ready to distrust mine eyes and wrangle with my reason that persuades me to any other trust but that I am mad; or else the lady's mad, yet if it were so, she could not sway her house.

Command her followers, take and give back affairs and their dispatch with such a smooth, discreet and stable bearing as I perceive she does, there's something in it that is deceiveable; but here the lady comes.

(Olivia and Priest enter)

Olivia: Blame not this haste of mine. If you mean well, now go with me and with this holy man into the chantry by, there, before him and underneath that consecrated roof, plight me the full assurance of your faith.

That my most jealous and too doubtful soul , may live at peace. He shall conceal it whiles you are willing it shall come to note, what time we will our celebration keep according to my birth.

What do you say?

Sebastian: I'll follow this good man, and go with you, and, having sworn truth, ever will be true.

Olivia: Then lead the way, good father; and heavens so shine, that they may fairly note this act of mine!

(Exeunt)

Act V, Scene 1

Before Olivia's house.

(Jester and Fabian enter)

Fabian: Now, as thou lovest me, let me see his letter.

Feste: Good Master Fabian, grant me another request.

Fabian: Anything.

Feste: Do not desire to see this letter.

Fabian: This is, to give a dog, and in recompense desire my dog again.

(Duke Orsino, Viola, Curio, and Lords enter)

Orsino: Belong you to the Lady Olivia, friends?

Feste: Ay, sir; we are some of her trappings.

Orsino: I know thee well; how dost thou, my good fellow?

Feste: Truly, sir, the better for my foes and the worse for my friends.

Orsino: Just the contrary, the better for thy friends.

Feste: No, sir, the worse.

Orsino: How can that be?

Feste: Merrily sir, they praise me and make an ass of me; now my foes tell me plainly I am an ass; so that by my foes sir I profit in the knowledge of myself, and by my friends, I am abused.

So that conclusions to be as kisses, if your four negatives make your two affirmatives; why then the worse for my friends and the better for my foes.

Orsino: Why, this is excellent.

Feste: By my troth, sir, no; though it please you to be one of my friends.

Orsino: Thou shalt not be the worse for me: there's gold.

Feste: But that it would be double-dealing, sir I would you could make it another.

Orsino: Oh, you give me ill counsel.

Feste: Put your grace in your pocket, sir, for this once, and let your flesh and blood obey it.

Orsino: Well, I will be so much a sinner, to be a double-dealer: there's another.

Feste: Primo, secundo, tertio, is a good play, and the old saying is, the third pays for all.

The triplex, sir, is a good tripping measure, or the bells of Saint Bennet; sir, may put you in mind, one, two, three.

Orsino: You can fool no more money out of me at this throw, if you will let your lady know I am here to speak with her, and bring her along with you, it may awake my bounty further.

Feste: Marry, sir, lullaby to your bounty till I come again.

I go, sir, but I would not have you to think that my desire of having is the sin of covetousness; but, as you say sir, let your bounty take a nap, I will awake it anon.

(Exits)

Viola: Here comes the man, sir, that did rescue me.

(Antonio and Officers enter)

Orsino: That face of his I do remember well, yet when I saw it last, it was besmeared as black as Vulcan in the smoke of war.

A bawbling vessel was he captain of, for shallow draught and bulk unprizable; with which such scathful grapple did he make with the most noble bottom of our fleet that very envy and the tongue of loss cried fame and honour on him.

What's the matter?

First Officer: Orsino, this is that Antonio, that took the Phoenix and her fraught from Candy; and this is he that did the Tiger board, when your young nephew Titus lost his leg.

Here in the streets, desperate of shame and state, in private brabble did we apprehend him.

Viola: He did me kindness sir, drew on my side, but in conclusion put strange speech upon me; I know not what it was but distraction.

Orsino: Notable pirate! thou salt-water thief!

What foolish boldness brought thee to their mercies, whom thou, in terms so bloody and so dear hast made thine enemies?

Antonio: Orsino, noble sir, be pleased that I shake off these names you give me.

Antonio never yet was thief or pirate, though I confess, on base and ground enough, Orsino's enemy.

A witchcraft drew me hither, that most ingrateful boy there by your side, from the rude sea's enraged and foamy mouth did I redeem; a wreck past hope he was.

His life I gave him and did thereto add my love, without retention or restraint, all his in dedication; for his sake did I expose myself, pure for his love into the danger of this adverse town.

Drew to defend him when he was beset where being apprehended, his false cunning, not meaning to partake with me in danger; taught him to face me out of his acquaintance, and grew a twenty years removed thing while one would wink, denied me mine own purse, which I had recommended to his use not half an hour before.

Viola: How can this be?

Orsino: When came he to this town?

Antonio: To-day, my lord; and for three months before, no interim, not a minute's vacancy; both day and night did we keep company.

(Enter **Olivia** and Attendants)

Orsino: Here comes the countess, now heaven walks on earth, but for thee; fellow, fellow, thy words are madness.

Three months this youth hath tended upon me, but more of that anon.

Take him aside.

Olivia: What would my lord, but that he may not have, wherein Olivia may seem serviceable?

Cesario, you do not keep promise with me.

Viola: Madam!

Orsino: Gracious Olivia

Olivia: What do you say, Cesario? Good my lord.

Viola: My lord would speak; my duty hushes me.

Olivia: If it be aught to the old tune, my lord, it is as fat and fulsome to mine ear as howling after music.

Orsino: Still so cruel?

Olivia: Still so constant, lord.

Orsino: What, to perverseness? You uncivil lady, to whose ingrate and unauspicious altars my soul the faithfull'st offerings hath breathed out that ever devotion tendered! What shall I do?

Olivia: Even what it please my lord, that shall become him.

Orsino: Why should I not, had I the heart to do it, like to the Egyptian thief at point of death, Kill what I love? A savage jealousy that sometimes savours nobly.

But hear me this, since you to non-regardance cast my faith, and that I partly know the instrument that screws me from my true place in your favour, live you the marble-breasted tyrant still; but this your minion, whom I know you love, and whom, by heaven I swear, I tender dearly, him will I tear out of that cruel eye where he sits crowned in his master's spite.

Come, boy, with me, my thoughts are ripe in mischief, I'll sacrifice the lamb that I do love, to spite a raven's heart within a dove.

Viola: And I, most jocund, apt and willingly, to do you rest a thousand deaths would die.

Olivia: Where goes Cesario?

Viola: After him I love more than I love these eyes, more than my life, more, by all mores, than ever I shall love wife.

If I do feign, you witnesses above punish my life for tainting of my love!

Olivia: Ay me, detested! How am I beguiled!

Viola: Who does beguile you? Who does do you wrong?

Olivia: Hast thou forgot thyself? Is it so long?

Call forth the holy father.

Orsino: Come, away!

Olivia: Whither, my lord? Cesario, husband, stay.

Orsino: Husband!

Olivia: Ay, husband: can he that deny?

Orsino: Her husband, sirrah!

iola: No, my lord, not I.

Olivia: Alas, it is the baseness of thy fear that makes thee strangle thy propriety.

Fear not, Cesario, take thy fortunes up, be that thou know'st thou art and then thou art as great as that thou fear'st.

(Priest enters)

Oh welcome father!

Father, I charge thee, by thy reverence here to unfold, though lately we intended to keep in darkness what occasion now reveals before it is ripe, what thou dost know hath newly passed between this youth and me.

Priest: A contract of eternal bond of love, confirmed by mutual joinder of your hands, attested by the holy close of lips, strengthened by interchangement of your rings; and all the ceremony of this compact sealed in my function, by my testimony.

Since when, my watch hath told me, toward my grave I have travelled but two hours.

Orsino: Oh thou dissembling cub! What wilt thou be when time hath sowed a grizzle on thy case? Or will not else thy craft so quickly grow, that thine own trip shall be thine overthrow?

Farewell, and take her; but direct thy feet where thou and I henceforth may never meet.

Viola: My lord, I do protest—

Olivia: Oh do not swear!

Hold little faith, though thou hast too much fear.

(Sir Andrew enter)

Sir Andrew Aguecheek: For the love of God, a surgeon!

Send one presently to Sir Toby.

Olivia: What's the matter?

Sir Andrew Aguecheek: He has broke my head across and has given Sir Toby a bloody coxcomb too; for the love of God, your help!

I had rather than forty pound I were at home.

Olivia: Who has done this, Sir Andrew?

Sir Andrew Aguecheek: The count's gentleman, one Cesario, we took him for a coward, but he's the very devil incardinate.

Orsino: My gentleman, Cesario?

Sir Andrew Aguecheek: Od's lifelings, here he is! You broke my head for nothing, and that that I did, I was set on to do it by Sir Toby.

Viola: Why do you speak to me? I never hurt you, you drew your sword upon me without cause; but I bespoke you fair, and hurt you not.

Sir Andrew Aguecheek: If a bloody coxcomb be a hurt, you have hurt me, I think you set nothing by a bloody coxcomb.

(Sir Toby Belch and Jester enter)

Here comes Sir Toby halting; you shall hear more, but if he had not been in drink, he would have tickled you othergates than he did.

Orsino: How now, gentleman! How is it with you?

Sir Toby Belch: That's all one has hurt me, and there's the end on it.

Sot, didst see Dick surgeon, sot?

Feste: Oh he's drunk, Sir Toby, an hour agone, his eyes were set at eight in the morning.

Sir Toby Belch: Then he's a rogue, and a passy measures pain, I hate a drunken rogue.

Olivia: Away with him! Who hath made this havoc with them?

Sir Andrew Aguecheek: I'll help you, Sir Toby, because well be dressed together.

Sir Toby Belch: Will you help? An ass-head and a coxcomb and a knave, a thin-faced knave, a gull!

Olivia: Get him to bed, and let his hurt be look'd to.

(Exeunt Jester, Fabian, Sir Toby Belch, and Sir Andrew)

(Sebastian enters)

Sebastian: I am sorry, madam, I have hurt your kinsman, but had it been the brother of my blood, I must have done no less with wit and safety.

You throw a strange regard upon me, and by that I do perceive it hath offended you, pardon me, sweet one, even for the vows we made each other but so late ago.

Orsino: One face, one voice, one habit, and two persons, a natural perspective, that is and is not!

Sebastian: Antonio, oh my dear Antonio!

How have the hours racked and tortured me, since I have lost thee!

Antonio: Sebastian are you?

Sebastian: Fear'st thou that, Antonio?

Antonio: How have you made division of yourself?

An apple, cleft in two, is not more twin than these two creatures.

Which is Sebastian?

Olivia: Most wonderful!

Sebastian: Do I stand there? I never had a brother, nor can there be that deity in my nature, of here and everywhere.

I had a sister whom the blind waves and surges have devoured.

Of charity, what kin are you to me? What countryman? What name? What parentage?

Viola: Of Messaline, Sebastian was my father, such a Sebastian was my brother too;so went he suited to his watery tomb.

If spirits can assume both form and suit you come to fright us.

Sebastian: A spirit I am indeed, but am in that dimension grossly clad which from the womb I did participate.

Were you a woman, as the rest goes even, I should my tears let fall upon your cheek, and say: Thrice-welcome, drowned Viola!

Viola: My father had a mole upon his brow.

Sebastian: And so had mine.

Viola: And died that day when Viola from her birth had numbered thirteen years.

Sebastian: Oh that record is lively in my soul!

He finished indeed his mortal act that day that made my sister thirteen years.

Viola: If nothing lets to make us happy both, but this my masculine usurped attire.

Do not embrace me till each circumstance of place, time, fortune, do cohere and jump that I am Viola, which to confirm I'll bring you to a captain in this town where lies my maiden weeds; by whose gentle help I was preserved to serve this noble count.

All the occurrence of my fortune since hath been between this lady and this lord.

Sebastian: (To Olivia) So comes it, lady, you have been mistook; but nature to her bias drew in that.

You would have been contracted to a maid, nor are you therein by my life, deceived, you are betrothrd both to a maid and man.

Orsino: Be not amazed; right noble is his blood.

If this be so, as yet the glass seems true, I shall have share in this most happy wreck.

(To Viola)

Boy, thou hast said to me a thousand times thou never shouldst love woman like to me.

Viola: And all those sayings will I overswear, and those swearings keep as true in soul as doth that orbed continent the fire that severs day from night.

Orsino: Give me thy hand, and let me see thee in thy woman's weeds.

Viola: The captain that did bring me first on shore hath my maid's garments; he upon some action as now in durance, at Malvolio's suit, a gentleman, and follower of my lady's.

Olivia: He shall enlarge him: fetch Malvolio hither, and yet alas, now I remember me,

they say poor gentleman he's much distracted.

(Jester re-enters with a letter, and Fabian)

A most extracting frenzy of mine own from my remembrance clearly banished his.

How does he, sirrah?

Feste: Truly, madam, he holds Belzebub at the staves's end as well as a man in his case may do, has here written a letter to you; I should have given it you to-day morning, but as a madman's epistles are no gospels, so it skills not much when they are delivered.

Olivia: Open it, and read it.

Feste: Look then to be well edified when the fool delivers the madman.

(Reads)

By the Lord, madam.

Olivia: How now! Art thou mad?

Feste: No, madam, I do but read madness, and your ladyship will have it as it ought to be, you must allow Vox.

Olivia: Pray to thee, read i' thy right wits.

Feste: So I do, Madonna; but to read his right wits is to read thus; therefore perpend my princess, and give ear.

Olivia: Read it you, sirrah.

(To Fabian)

Fabian: (Reads) By the Lord, madam, you wrong me, and the world shall know it, though you have put me into darkness and given your drunken cousin rule over me, yet have I the benefit of my senses as well as your ladyship.

I have your own letter that induced me to the semblance I put on, with the which I doubt not but to do myself much right, or you much shame.

Think of me as you please, I leave my duty a little unthought of and speak out of my injury.

The Madly-Used Malvolio.

Olivia: Did he write this?

Feste: Ay, madam.

Orsino: This savours not much of distraction.

Olivia: See him delivered, Fabian; bring him hither.

(Exit Fabian)

My lord so please you, these things further thought on, to think me as well a sister as a wife, one day shall crown the alliance on it, so please you, here at my house and at my proper cost.

Orsino: Madam, I am most apt to embrace your offer.

(To Viola)

Your master quits you; and for your service done him, so much against the mettle of your sex, so far beneath your soft and tender breeding, and since you called me master for so long here is my hand.

You shall from this time be your master's mistress.

Olivia: A sister! You are she.

(Fabian, with Malvolio re-enter)

Orsino: Is this the madman?

Olivia: Ay, my lord, this same.

How now, Malvolio!

Malvolio: Madam, you have done me wrong, notorious wrong.

Olivia: Have I, Malvolio? no.

Malvolio: Lady, you have. Pray you, peruse that letter.

You must not now deny it is your hand, write from it, if you can, in hand or phrase;

or say it is not your seal, nor your invention.

You can say none of this, well, grant it then and tell me in the modesty of honour, why you have given me such clear lights of favour, bade me come smiling and cross-gartered to you to put on yellow stockings and to frown upon Sir Toby and the lighter people.

Upon acting this in an obedient hope, why have you suffered me to be imprisoned, kept in a dark house, visited by the priest and made the most notorious geck and gull that ever invention played on? Tell me why.

Olivia: Alas, Malvolio, this is not my writing, though I confess, much like the character; but out of question 'tis Maria's hand.

And now I do bethink me, it was she first told me thou was it mad, then camest in smiling, and in such forms which here were presupposed upon thee in the letter.

Pray to thee, be content, this practice hath most shrewdly passed upon thee; but when we know the grounds and authors of it, thou shalt be both the plaintiff and the judge of thine own cause.

Fabian: Good madam, hear me speak, and let no quarrel nor no brawl to come taint the condition of this present hour, which I have wondered at.

In hope it shall not, most freely I confess, myself and Toby set this device against Malvolio here upon some stubborn and uncourteous part we had conceived against him.

Maria wrote the letter at Sir Toby's great importance in recompense whereof he hath married her.

How with a sportful malice it was followed, may rather pluck on laughter than revenge if that the injuries be justly weighed that have on both sides passed.

Olivia: Alas, poor fool, how have they baffled thee!

Feste: Why, some are born great, some achieve greatness, and some have greatness thrown upon them.

I was one, sir, in this interlude, one Sir Topas sir, but that's all one.

By the Lord, fool, I am not mad, but do you remember?

Madam, why laugh you at such a barren rascal? And you smile not, he's gagged, and thus the whirligig of time brings in his revenges.

Malvolio: I'll be revenged on the whole pack of you.

(Exits)

Olivia: He hath been most notoriously abused.

Orsino: Pursue him and entreat him to a peace, he hath not told us of the captain yet, when that is known and golden time convents.

A solemn combination shall be made of our dear souls, meantime, sweet sister we will not part from hence.

Cesario, come, for so you shall be, while you are a man; but when in other habits you are seen Orsino's mistress and his fancy's queen.

(Exeunt all, except Jester)

Feste: (Sings)

When that I was and a little tiny boy, with hey, oh, the wind and the rain, a foolish thing was but a toy; for the rain it raineth every day.

But when I came to man's estate, with hey, oh, & against knaves and thieves men shut their gate, for the rain, but when I came, alas! To wife,

With hey, ho, & by swaggering could I never thrive, for the rain; but when I came unto my beds with hey, ho, with toss-pots still had drunken heads,

For the rain, a great while ago, began the world.

With hey, ho, but that's all one, our play is done, we'll strive to please you every day. **(Exits)**

The End

Description of Titles

The Comedy of Errors
Caught in a land of embittered woman and war, caught in months of strife, where a merchant's visit offers little natural relief. The fleeting moment of approving gold, inspire further bitterness, upon an approach to the marketplace, and then the women that occupy within them.

19 Characters

The Taming of the Shrew
Arrangements are made to spencer would be suiters to melt the splendors of a strong willed women. The winning is found pledged, influencing maids to seek their turns, and meanwhile terms required, an authentic spirit that they will/would wed soon.

34 Characters

Love's Labor's Lost
The house of a scholarly pursuit, returns into an expressive, either poetic or drunken as highlighting the gold-slur filled house of charms and dance like rhymes

19 Characters

A Midsummer Night's Dream
Journey into a land of fairies, where creatures are found to have the same issues as nobilities. Exemplifying, perhaps, there's no place like home. Meet fairies as they frolic and play the noble hearts and sway, posed in the recesses of night, and mystic lands of a faraway kingdom.

22 Characters

The Merchant of Venice

An angry Shylock brings to trial a merchant, over a lover's quarrel disrupted, demanding pounds of flesh. With no desires for even three times the amount, the Shylock demands his vengeance at heart.

22 Characters

The Merry Wives of Windsor
Mistresses and lords try and relate towards one another, as various important community figures come to have their word/seek the hostesses. Pleasantries are exchanged as a range of charms are expressed, until conversation resembled so to folly.

23 Characters

Much Ado About Nothing
Soldiery level consideration occupy the gossip, as several hostilities are summoned up, onto heart related matter. Also in conflict. The latter portion of the story lightens up to a women's home and pleasantries. Thereafter, a general search and care in actions, creating response phrasing poetic to the responses of leadership parading, until an end full of sensitivity asking gently questions, onto kisses

23 Characters

As You Like It
Troubled lower nobles venture about daily business, with some mild graces towards the ladies found. In need of relief or play, the Duke and family members take to the woods, where jests of drinking turn into troubled amusements, or warmth of a women's heart.

26 Characters

Troilus and Cressida
The infamous Greek battle for Troy. A large army arrives to take back the lost love of a humiliated foe. Both sides mobilize heroes onto the field, as soldiers and generals move to the side, and let strategies and fate take their course.

21+ Characters

All's Well That Ends Well
A tale of delightful, womanly gossip of a prestigious sort, until the French King has his word on the excellence of others. The story initially revolves around a strong willed countess, whose courteous pose and insight, reflect a nobility reflective of the house and court (council). Dialogue therein revolving around the councils rather, to exemplify (court counselling women).

25 Characters

Measure for Measure
Statesmen discourse leading with time to a personal reflection. Strolling Dukes and strong willed women occupy the background, where high-function status and family discourse intertwine within formalities (of administrative foresight, expression) observed.

24 Characters

Richard III
An in palace drama with King Richard the 3rd, Queen Elizabeth, and Queen Margret. Onto a haunting reunion, as the state processes royal executions.

61+ Characters

The Life and Death of King John
King John and Queen Elinor entertain the royal court, where a bastard has come to make his day. Strategic deployments of influence are exemplified, as the bastard plots about until alerts, alarm corruption has delivered trouble makers known.

24 Characters

Romeo and Juliet
Lovers emerge within a city gripped with two feuding houses apposed. As turmoil are caught in bitter heat, the lover's. Bliss and undying pledge becomes them, onto the eternal soul (of love and romance).

33 Characters

Othello
A hopeful Othello calls upon the favor of allies based on proposed merits, which called upon allies and foes to him. In a mixed response, allies and foes campaign both against Othello, becoming a bitter, personal tangle over a mislead love adventure representing the future of either fates

25 Characters

Macbeth
A desperate Macbeth ventures towards witches to tell fortune, returning to a castle haunted by ghost/old-spirits. Macbeth's worries become frightful nightmares, along the despair of the household around him.

39 Characters

Mark Antony and Cleopatra
The relations or affections of Mark Anthony and Cleopatra, onto the strategic interactions between Mark Anthony and Octavius. The discourse moves to the Octavius house, revealing Octavia, and later then, Pompey in the background. Overall the focus retains upon Mark Anthony, Cleopatra, and Octavius.

56+ Characters

Coriolanus
Citizens riot during a famine, while the state administrative intervenes and otherwise discourses the seriousness of the matter and war. Lady's calm the general ambience, until the sword is mobilized to defend the gates, , while the plight of people is nevertheless heard convincing Roman elites the problem is being found/fought within.

60 Characters

Pericles Prince of Tyre
A thoughtful/reflective Pericles interposes his good will and well-meaning nature, which leads him to visit fishermen friends, and onto state function. Pericles is then confronted, required to (take a plunge) to marry, embedding him deeper into ocean stock of sea life among sailors experience and merchant owners, investing his interest as babe, securing his destiny as then, future king

44 Characters

Cymbeline
Cymbeline, friend or loyalist to the first Caesars, is summoned into battle. Meanwhile there are personal matters to attend to within the noble house.

41 Characters

The Winter's Tale
A gossipy tale of high office, administrative daily insight onto the tender meaning of things and people an how they unite unwittingly at the discourse of their respected hierarchies of partnership. Profoundness therein inspiring the recounts of clown and child, as examples perhaps of what state administration and or nobility's company keeps.

34+ Characters

The Tempest
After an earth shattering storm, a fairy dwelling world is found. There magic and graces are there in song, glory and praises.

21 Characters

The Two Gentlemen of Verona
Loving beginnings, yet far too. General virtues going upwards in hierarchies, with overall chivalrous wits.

Twelfth Night
An evening in the company of sound gatherings, seemingly a docile manner recount version of noble delights. In similarities of the pose, composing an environment of insight and oversight.

Henry the 8th
Across chamber and palace, Dukes and lords, until Queen Katharine's and King Henry VIII's present their graces, conversing the Cardinal then. The signs then, an Elizabeth is born.

Richard II
King Richard the 2nd readies the armed forces at the sound of alarm, while later Henry IV is near for discussion. King Richard the 2nd and his groom.

Henry V
King Henry the 5th, as found across his palace, until a readiness for war. King Henry the 5th and the French King, with armies both have at it.

Henry VI, Part 1
Funeral of King Henry the 5th, Henry VI makes his approach to France. Henry VI fashions as thy lord protector.

Henry VI, Part 2
King Henry the 6th, where the Cardinal is seen mocking protectors with praise, as all the rage. Queen Margaret at King Henry VI, until the end.

Henry VI, Part 3
King Henry VI is busy fighting a succession of battles, France and England as having at it, yet again.

King Henry the 5th
King Henry 5 fight his way toward France, they reach the peaceful and loving responses of a French King.

Henry IV, Part 1
King Henry the 4th, from Palace to Pub, onto the battle fields again. Until there is no rebellion.

Henry IV, Part 2
Henry IV, from Palace, Priest and then tavern, he nevertheless finds some peace, after reflection. King Henry IV, and then King Henry V as fashionable by the end.

Titus Andronicus
A story of Romans and Goths, where roman sways give way. And then to see about Goths and proving worthiness.

28 Characters

Julius Caesar
Near the Final days of the 1st Caesar, and the continuation everlasting as through Octavius.

Hamlet
Hamlet, and his father the King, the father yet a Ghost. Hamlet, not so eager to join.

King Lear
King Lear, from palace to castle, to fighting the French in the field. After battle King Lear is in bed, the Doctor discourses, what lays then now, will have an impact upon the end.

Timon of Athens
A story set in Greece, a place of poets and cultured, good graces. From Arts and daily expressive, to political and charmed.

www.ingramcontent.com/pod-product-compliance
Lightning Source LLC
Chambersburg PA
CBHW071454080526
44587CB00014B/2109